ENDORSEMENTS FOR
THE GOSPEL ACCORDING TO BREAKING BAD

"As a fan of *Breaking Bad*, and as a student of religion and popular culture, it's now clear to me that I haven't been paying close enough attention to the series' moral and spiritual dimensions. Thanks to *The Gospel According to Breaking Bad*, I won't make that mistake again."

— **Mark I. Pinsky, religion journalist and author of**
The Gospel According to The Simpsons

"One of the better *Gospel According To*'s I've read and I think I've read most of them."

— **Cathleen Falsani Possley, religion journalist and author of**
The Dude Abides: The Gospel According to the Coen Brothers

"Blake Atwood is one of the most thoughtful Christians you'll meet. He's always dreaming up new ideas and projects. In *The Gospel According to Breaking Bad*, Blake applies his mind to yet another endeavor by taking a unique look at the spiritual elements of this popular TV show. You've likely never read anything quite like it."

— **Jonathan Merritt, Senior Columnist for Religion News Service and author of** *Jesus is Better Than You Imagined*

"Many of the best theological conversations are being held on and around television shows like *Breaking Bad*. Blake Atwood offers a distinctly Christian perspective on the themes and issues this landmark show discusses. *The Gospel According to Breaking Bad* is provocative, compelling, smart and a whole lot of fun. I absolutely love this sort of serious and respectful engagement with popular culture, and I desperately hope Blake's labor of love inspires a multitude of spin-offs."

— **J.R. Forasteros, Pastor at Beavercreek Church of the Nazarene, Blogger, Host of the Storymen Podcast**

"Blake Atwood's book is different from many 'gospel according to' books in that it's not just a pop culture gimmick to shove the gospel down the reader's throat. Rather, his thoughtful, substantive examination of this brilliant show helps us all—Christian or not—consider the world around us and the media we engage with a more critical moral and theological lens."

— Christian Piatt, Creator and Editor of the 'Banned Questions' books and author of *postChristian* (Aug. 2014) and *PregMANcy*

"By putting Walter White and company under the microscope, Atwood brings the elemental structure of the human soul into magnified clarity. Who knew a world of drug kingpins, pathological liars and narcissistic grandiosity could be so ripe with moral meaning? Examining Vince Gilligan's post-modern tale of pilgrim's regress through a gospel lens enables Atwood to offer up a redemptive future for all of us who live east of Eden. This is a must-read guide for all *Breaking Bad* fans who want to savor the final season as it unfolds.

— Brad Russell, Senior Editor at FaithVillage.com

"In *The Gospel According to Breaking Bad*, Blake Atwood brings a fan's passion, a critic's analysis and a Christian's perspective to bear on the most provocative television program in recent memory. If you find the show intriguing, perplexing or just plain compelling, you'll want to read this book. Spoiler alert: You'll find yourself in these pages."

— Marv Knox, Publisher, The Baptist Standard

The Gospel According to *Breaking Bad*

BLAKE ATWOOD

*TO MY OTHER FAVORITE
W.W.
IT'S AN HONOUR
WORKING WITH YOU.
FONDLY
G.B.*

DONATION
10% of the proceeds from the sale of this ebook are being
donated to Oak Ridge Disciple House in Florence, TX.
"The Oak Ridge Disciple House is a non-profit, faith-based,
Christian character-building ministry geared towards reaching
men who are broken from drug and alcohol addictions."

Learn more at www.oakridgedisciplehouse.com.

ISBN: 978-0-9897773-1-5

Published by AtWords Press

Edited by Alise Wright

Illustrations by Wes Molebash

AUTHOR'S NOTE
regarding this print edition

The first edition of *The Gospel According to Breaking Bad* was written and released as an ebook prior to the airing of the show's final eight episodes. Consequently, in the following pages you will read questions that have been answered and hypotheticals that have proven to be true, or, more likely, false.

Part of the popular allure of the show, especially as it careened toward its epic conclusion, was the rampant postulation of how it was all going to end. The Internet exploded with possible end-game scenarios for Walter White, some of which proved to be ridiculous, but a few of which proved to be rather prescient. A few such guesses, including my own, are recorded here.

Following the series' conclusion, I intended to rewrite much of the text that questioned the ending of the show. However, I've left many of my questions and postulations intact. In writing the last chapter, an update that was released following the series finale, I discovered that my expectations of the show's ending changed how I interpreted *Breaking Bad* as a whole.

As great art often does, the show placed a mirror in front of me, revealing more about myself than I ever wanted to discover.

1. **"My name is Walter Hartwell White."**   **1**
   Breaking into *Breaking Bad*

2. **"Say my name!"**   **15**
   Who's who in the ABQ

3. **"Blue, yellow, pink, whatever man."**   **33**
   A spectrum of possibilities

4. **"Lung cancer. Inoperable."**   **43**
   Death: the one who also knocks

5. **"Better call Saul!"**   **61**
   Justifying the unjust

6. **"I am the one who knocks!"**   **73**
   Heisenberg's hell-bent hubris

7. **"I have made a series of very bad decisions."**   **93**
   Fate vs. free will

8. **"He was a problem dog."**   **103**
   Jesse's breaking good

9. **"You're a drug dealer."**   **113**
   Meth as metaphor

10. **"What does a man do, Walter?"**   **131**
    The Gospel According to *Breaking Bad*

11. **"I'm in the empire business."**   **147**
    How *Breaking Bad* could have ended

12. **"You want them to actually miss you."**   **159**
    How *Breaking Bad* actually ended and
    why the finale changed everything

"My name is Walter Hartwell White."

An Introduction Like No Other

THOUGH I DON'T question your fandom of the show, allow me to remind you of *Breaking Bad*'s very first scene, a breakneck *in media res* opening unlike anything else ever depicted on TV. Like a user's first hit, the instantly memorable introduction to the fascinating universe of *Breaking Bad* hooked viewers from the very beginning. In fact, the first page of the script caused Bryan Cranston to sign on to become Walter White.[1]

Breaking Bad opens on cacti in the southwest United States, cuts to light streaking across a rock formation, then follows the flight path of a personless pair of pants as they descend to the road below, only for a speeding, careening Winnebago on the lam to crush them into the dirt.

Clad in a gas mask and tightey-whiteys, our supposed hero drives the RV in frantic desperation. Through quick cuts, we see why: someone in the passenger seat, also wearing a gas mask but much more fully clothed, lies motionless. Two just-as-lifeless bodies slide around on some sort of dark liquid in the back of the RV, strewn about as it is with chemistry equipment.

As the driver's gas mask fogs up, the RV slides off the dirt road and the mobile chem lab deathtrap nosedives into the ditch. Stumbling out of the Winnebago, he peels off the gas mask and promptly suffers an apparent anxiety attack, but not without taking the measured though seemingly unnecessary step of putting a green button-up shirt back on. Sucking in a mouthful of air, he runs back into the RV, grabs a gun from one of the presumed-dead bodies, then retrieves his wallet and a video camera from the glove box.

Once back outside, he records what he believes may be his last will and testament to a soundtrack of approaching sirens:

My name is Walter Hartwell White. I live at 308 Negra Arroyo Lane, Albuquerque, New Mexico, 87104. To all law enforcement entities, this is not an admission of guilt. I am speaking to my family now. [He covers the camera with his hand, preventing future viewers from seeing tears in his eyes. He gathers himself before continuing.] Skyler, you are the love of my life. I hope you know that. Walter Jr., you're my big man. There are, there are going to be some . . . things . . . things that you'll come to learn about me in the next few days. I just want you to know that, no matter how it makes me look, I only had you in my heart. [He looks behind himself]. Goodbye.

As sirens intensify, Walter places his wallet and the videocamera on the ground. His demeanor instantly changes from heartbroken to steeled determination. The camera pans behind Walter as he pulls the gun he'd tucked into the backside of his underwear. He steps into the middle of the road like Billy the Kid at high noon. Pantsless but uncaring, he aims the gun at whomever's been following him.

Cut to black.

Roll title credits.

Close agape jaw.

THE FIRST HIT

There are times in life when you know you're witnessing something better than normal. A small voice inside says, *This could be really good. I should give it a chance.* Maybe it's a book, a show, or even a relationship, but there's a hint of greatness in it that your soul can almost taste. It's those certain moments in life you wish you could revisit for the specific reason of being able to experience *that thing* like it was the first time you ever experienced it. You might even equate it to chasing the window, but we'll get to that in time.

I wish I could recall my thoughts when I first watched the pilot episode for AMC's *Breaking Bad* on January 20, 2008. Was I enthralled with the series from the outset? Did I think it was the best show on television then? Did I enjoy the acting, the plot, or the cinematography most in the premiere episode? Was I fearful that the show was too dark, even for cable TV, hopelessly set for a one-season run, grateful for an overdose of critical acclaim but killed off due to popular rejection? Could I see that hours upon hours of my life were about to be willingly hijacked by a meth-dealing chemistry teacher and his loser, stoner apprentice? Did I know that I'd just taken my first hit of a highly addictive substance *and I liked it*?

Unfortunately, I didn't record my thoughts from that time. What I do know is that the show continually grew more impressive in its acting, writing, plot, and intensity. Nearly every episode somehow managed to ratchet the stakes to an absurd though still believable degree while causing my jaw to actually drop in shock. My increasing infatuation with the show caused me to wonder:

• Why am I so taken with this television series that's so far removed from my normal life?

• Why do I care so much for these already broken individuals bent on breaking further, drowning in the murky waters of their own moral choices?

• Why am I shocked when even well-intentioned monsters behave like monsters?

• Why do I rejoice when bad things happen to bad people?

• Why do I wait for Walter's redemption?

Through five terrifyingly suspenseful seasons, I've actually sat on the edge of my seat as an episode concludes, hoping against hope that *this would be the time that Walt makes everything right,* only to see him regress deeper into a Scarface-worshipping life of crime and power-hungry madness that's all too real for his family, friends and ~~co-workers~~ co-cookers.

What is it about this innocent everyman who turns to making and distributing meth that so engages me? What is it about his former student and current apprentice Jesse that makes me root for *him* to be the one redeemed in the end? Why do the intricate plot lines, so gorgeously shot and meticulously, patiently set in motion, cause me to question what I'd do in similar situations? How do such grand, ancient themes like justice, vengeance, pride, and death find their way into a 21st century black comedy drama set in Albuquerque, New Mexico?

How can something as bright as "the gospel" shine forth in such a dark show?

While coming alongside me to search for answers to these questions, I implore you, whether you've already broken bad or not, to consider this book much like I did the opening episode: *This could be really good. I should give it a chance.*

Also, here's a warning to any reader who hasn't watched the entirety of *Breaking Bad*: stop reading. This book has more spoilers than a classic car convention. If you want to enjoy the show without knowing major plot points, proceed no further. Go watch the series, then come back and dig deeper into the show with this book. I'll wait.

THE WORST IDEA

Breaking Bad should never have been made. A middle-aged, middle-class protagonist receives a death sentence in the pilot episode. This unlikely anti-hero then turns to a life of hard crime by cooking crystal meth. After hearing the pitch for the show, Sony's Michael Lynton told Vince Gilligan it was "the single worst idea for a television series I've ever heard in my life."[2] *Weeds*, a show that also fixates on drug-dealing to assist the family, was about to debut on Showtime. The landscape of television in 2008 had not seen or heard of anything like *Breaking Bad*, as anyone who's watched the pilot can attest.

What network in their right mind would take such a chance? A network drunk on the runaway success of their first original series.

Just a year prior to *Breaking Bad*'s debut, AMC aired *Mad Men*, a riveting period-piece set in a 1960s advertising agency. *Mad Men* follows the adulterous exploits of the dashing Don Draper and features the rapidly transforming culture of the 60s as nearly a character unto itself. AMC reveled in both critical and popular success with *Mad Men*, a show which garnered the network four consecutive Emmys for Outstanding Drama Series for each of its first four seasons.[3]

According to TV critic and author Alan Sepinwall, AMC received multitudes of pitches for period dramas due to *Mad Men*'s success. But, smartly, AMC ran as far away as they could from their tentpole series. What better way to showcase their diversity of content than to contrast the hip, suave, 60s chic look with a man in his underwear in the desert? They greenlit *Breaking Bad*, a thoroughly modern—even postmodern—show, much to the surprise and delight of creator Vince Gilligan.[4]

The television landscape of the late 2000s was about to be submerged in dark shades of White and crystal blue.

THE MORAL UNIVERSE OF BREAKING BAD

Show creator Vince Gilligan encapsulated the morality of *Breaking Bad* in a *New York Times* interview from 2011:

If there's a larger lesson to *Breaking Bad*, it's that actions have consequences. If religion is a reaction of man, and nothing more, it seems to me that it represents a human desire for wrongdoers to be punished. I hate the idea of Idi Amin living in Saudi Arabia for the last 25 years of his life. That galls me to no end. I feel some sort of need for biblical atonement, or justice, or something. I like to believe there is some comeuppance, that karma kicks in at some point, even if it takes years or decades to happen. My girlfriend says this great thing that's become my philosophy as well. 'I want to believe there's a heaven. But I can't not believe there's a hell.'[5]

As a one-time Catholic school acolyte himself, Gilligan understands judgment and the eternal battle of good and evil. Through the lens of his show, we may be provided a glimpse into his belief system, but I'd posit that *Breaking Bad* reveals more about American beliefs as a whole than Gilligan's singular and fascinating 44-minute long visions.

In fact, in the interview cited above, reporter David Segal relates how the show struck a chord with the everyman. Unlike *Mad Men*, AMC's other popular show that debuted to wide audiences in 2008, *Breaking Bad's* top three viewing cities were Albuquerque/Santa Fe, Kansas City, and Memphis. Typically, higher-rated shows enjoy huge market share in New York City and Los Angeles, the entertainment meccas of America. To Segal, this appears to make Gilligan "TV's first true red-state auteur. His characters lead middle American lives in a middle-American place, and they are beset with middle-American problems. They speak like middle Americans too, and they inhabit a realm of moral ambiguities that's overseen by a man with both a wicked sense of humor and a highly refined sense of right and wrong."

In 2011, cultural commentator Chuck Klosterman posited why he thinks *Breaking Bad* to be the best series on TV, beating out such notable series as *The Wire*, *The Sopranos*, and *Mad Men*. "There's one profound difference between this series and the other three, and it has to do with its handling of morality: *Breaking Bad* is the only one built on the uncomfortable premise that there's an irrefutable difference between what's right and what's wrong, and it's the only one where the characters have real control over how they choose to live."[6]

Writ large, *Breaking Bad* is a postmodern morality play. In other words, it's an anti-morality play. This isn't to say that the show is amoral—far from it—but it is to say that the predetermined conclusion of a morality play, the redemption of its protagonist, is not going to occur by series end. Gilligan said as much when he related his goal for the series: to see "Mr. Chips turn into Scarface." Ironically enough, a British *evangelical* newspaper first published the story *Goodbye, Mr. Chips*, a work that recounts the modest pursuits of a goody-two-shoes schoolteacher. In contrasting such a serene character with Tony Montana from *Scarface*, a fictional character who has become the literal poster boy for power, prestige, and violence, Gilligan set out an immense task for himself. How low can he make Walter White go? In order to accomplish this drastic and never-before-done-on-TV transformation, he would have to attack Walter with two of the greatest temptations this world offers: money and power.

In medieval morality plays, actors portrayed certain virtues

[handwritten margin note: Not really though – 2's just a tragedy]

and vices, fighting for the soul of the hero. Since these types of plays are believed to have been created by 13th century monks, the play's simple three-part structure should come as no surprise:

1. An innocent man comes onto the stage.
2. The man falls into temptation, fighting The World, The Flesh, and the Devil.
3. The man repents of his wrongdoing and turns to God for help.

Within the first four minutes of the very first episode, we're shown that this man is definitely not going to give up. Half-naked and wielding a gun, he waits patiently for the sirens to arrive, determined to have his own "Say hello to my little friend" moment.

So why do I think redemption is still possible within the world of *Breaking Bad*?

MY MORAL UNIVERSE

Because I believe that *anyone* can be redeemed, even the irrepressible, seemingly irredeemable Walter White. You may think this an absurd statement, but an understanding of my background may help you rationalize such a ridiculous claim.

When reading a work of non-fiction, especially one that espouses a particular point of view, I find it helpful to know more about the slants, biases, and bents of the author. To that end, allow me to share about my own upbringing and views on life. To some, this story may be all too familiar. To others, it may be wholly alien, or even demonized. Regardless, I share a part of my own story because what I believe is intrinsic to the words you'll be reading in this work, that is, should you choose to proceed any further.[7]

Above all, I identify as a Christian. While my actions and words may not always signify that fact, I believe that Jesus Christ was fully a real man and equally the Son of God, a divine being purposely sent to earth to free us from the sad predicament we've created for ourselves. I believe in the Gospel, that the only way for me to fully experience life both now and in the hereafter is to give up my life to the one who gave me life in the first place. More than just an intellectual nodding of the head to the words I heard preached every Sunday while growing up, I'm now old enough to explain moments of palpable interaction with a loving, caring, and near God. I am a Christian because I believe the old, old story. I am also a Christian because I've heard the narrator of that story speak directly into my life.

Raised in the Bible belt by a God-fearing single mother and grandparents I consider prime examples of Christian love, I attended a Baptist church often, even on Sunday nights, when the *truly* saved attended.[8] I learned the Baptist moral code more through osmosis than anything else. I didn't drink, do drugs, have sex, or swear. Many Christians can identify with this type of rules-based existence. For me, it led to pride for my good behavior, an earnest belief that my good works could merit me more favor with God. This was a wildly errant view of the gospel, but we'll get to that later. Suffice it to say that, though all my outer actions appeared morally respectable, my inner nature was still a stronghold of pride, selfishness, and sin.

During my formative spiritual years, I shied away from "The World." This is the biblical terminology that Christians would use, plucked from Jesus' words in John 17:16. "The World" was a scary place, where divorced alcoholics would cuss at their prostitute girlfriends to ply you with drugs if you even made eye contact. I say this facetiously, but there was a part of my brain at that time which knew the road to hell was smooth, and one false step could lead me to eternal damnation. Like any good Baptist kid, I attempted to fill that cultural void with its Christian counterparts. This amounted to reading much by C.S. Lewis, actually subscribing to *Contemporary Christian Music Magazine*,[9] and going to church just about any time its doors were open.[10]

Then I fell in love with a crass, yellow family.[11]

The Simpsons were culturally astute despite the dad's seeming stupidity. They made fun of my religion, but not really. They made me laugh, constantly. Those crafty cartoon devils even arrived at my house every Sunday night, beckoning me to stay home, bent on ruining my relationship with God. I'd suffer the plaintive cries of my mom, "You shouldn't be watching that show." I'd nod in agreement, but the channel wouldn't change.

Who knew that my first slide on the slippery road to hell would be encouraged by cheers of "Cowabunga?" Why did I not know that "the world" was hilarious, entertaining, enticing, and, dare I say it, enjoyable? I surely wouldn't lose my salvation due to a bratty fictional character, right?

I learned three things through my decades-long love affair with *The Simpsons*: always retire at the top of your game, it's OK to laugh at yourself, and "The World" is not a place to fear.

What does all of this have to do with *The Gospel According to Breaking Bad?* For starters, Mark Pinsky's *The Gospel According to the Simpsons* inspired this book, and his work is a fascinating glimpse into one of the most surprisingly spiritual shows of our time. Secondly, it's important for me to include a few disclaimers up front.

Breaking Bad deals with intense issues: death, drugs, violence, gangs, murder, etc. While I know many who have suffered the devastation of death or cancer or divorce, the world of *Breaking Bad* is often foreign to me. What I know about the effects of drug usage stems from the show and whatever after-school specials I may have seen years ago. Part of the genesis of this book deals with the question as to why I'm so enamored with a show that is so wholly different from my everyday life. I assume (and would *greatly* hope) that your world is quite different from Walter's, but possibly one of the most fascinating things about this show is that Walter starts out just like you and me, or at least like someone we know. He is an Everyman we can all relate to, but can we relate to who he becomes?

Some Christians may assume I'm condoning the actions as seen in the show. That's a ridiculous assumption. While *Breaking Bad* is often an intensely violent show, it pales in comparison to the shocking and oftentimes confusing amount of violence as depicted in the Bible.[12] *Breaking Bad* uses violence for dramatic effect, to hold the viewer in rapt attention, as well as to move plot lines forward. Additionally, it's a tragic depiction of the shocking violence that occurs on an hourly basis throughout our very real world. This book does not seek to celebrate violence, as our culture suffers from that media madness already, but to ask why such violence is necessary in Walter's world, and whether or not Walter's actions, or anyone else's for the matter, can ever redeem him.

"The World" is not something to be feared or a place to flee. Popular scholarship holds that the Essenes, a Judaic sect, fled to Qumran in the 1st century in order to live a more spiritual life. While much internal good can stem from such a monastic life, one half of the equation goes missing by default: giving of yourself to others. By entering into "The World" (but reminding yourself that you're not "of the world"), a Christian can look at popular culture through a critical lens that appreciates its beauty and truthfulness while also witnessing its longing for redemption. If you're lost, this will be fleshed out in a later chapter. Suffice it to say that a careful Christian can consume popular culture without fearing it poisoning their soul.

To sum: I'm a Christian. I know that this term carries many different types of baggage, loaded with millennia of historical weight, as well as your own personal history with those who call themselves "Christians." Whether a Christian yourself or not, I ask you to engage this work with an open mind. My aim is to provide both interesting insight into the show as well as a glimpse into what the show can tell us about ourselves.

I love *Breaking Bad*. In the long line of my fascination with the well-told stories of popular culture, *Breaking Bad* ranks as one of the best narrative journeys I've ever embarked upon.

I'm a Christian and I love *Breaking Bad*. These are not mutually exclusive statements, though the first statement greatly affects the second. This is what you have to know before proceeding.

But enough about me.

Let's talk about our mutual friend Walt.

"Say my name!"

"YOU'RE HEISENBERG."

FOR GOOD OR ill, names define us. We can refuse to carry the mantle that accompanies our name or we can strive as valiantly as possible to live up to the name given us. While some may never give second thought to the meaning behind their name, writers often give careful consideration to their characters' names. After all, it's a person they'll have to live with for a long time. By delving into the meaning and origin of the names encountered in *Breaking Bad*, we can learn much about who these people are, who they might become, and who they were all along.

Gilligan and his talented crew of writers couldn't have been more blatant in their intentions to have the audience emotionally identify with *Breaking Bad*'s protagonist. By christening Walter with the last name of White, we're predisposed to a myriad of notions when it comes to his identity. He's a blank canvas, allowing us to paint our own issues into his world. He's an everyman, necessary but inconsequential. He's a decent man, working as hard as he can to provide for his family.

What's the first word that comes to mind when you think "white?" For me, as a kid sure to be at church nearly every weekend singing hymns that proclaim Jesus' ability to make me "white as snow," the word "pure" springs to mind. Unblemished and untarnished, the word "white" connotes goodness, wholeness, and holiness, a word that means "set apart."[13] By supplying Walter with such a sterling surname, we may be subconsciously acquiescing to Walter's perceived inherent goodness.

While the vast majority of us can't relate to the utterly unique opening sequence of the pilot episode, its subsequent scenes may be all too familiar: exercising at home, breakfast with the family, dropping a kid off at school, tolerating a day job, enduring a second job to make ends meet, attending a surprise birthday party, cautiously expecting a baby. One of the most gripping aspects of this show is in its portrayal of the absurd amongst the mundane. The domestic scenes keep the plot grounded in real life, while simultaneously coercing us to identify with Walter White. We know him because we are him, or, at the very least, we know someone who could easily be him.

Gilligan also liked the name Walter White "because of the alliterative sound of it and because it's strangely bland, yet sticks in your head nonetheless—you know, white is the color of vanilla, of blandness."[14] In other words, he wanted to portray an everyman who's more likely to blend into the background than to be the center of attention. Despite its blandness, the name sticks inside your mind. Walter White has become one of the most well-known characters in recent TV history. Why is that?

Before even knowing his story, and whether we're aware of the way his simple name has worked its way into our minds, we've likely already formed a positive opinion of Walter. When we learn of his cancer, his pregnant wife, and his son that endures cerebral palsy, we're forcibly shoved over the precipice of non-involvement with this seemingly timid chemistry teacher. We begin to root for him, at least until we discover that Walter White may be one of the most impure men ever depicted on TV.

Then again, if we knew our German a little better, we would know where Walter is leading us. From the German *wald* for "rule" and *hari* for "army," Walter means "ruler of the army." As we're well aware of by Season 5, Walter commands his own army through creative, intelligent, devious manipulations. In Walter's mind, he quite lives up to his name: a pure ruler. The pre-season ad for Season 5 admits as much, as we see hazmat-suited Walter perched on a lawn chair, mountains of meth behind him, a cascade of cash beside him, with the simple phrase "ALL HAIL THE KING" floating like a thought-bubble above his unmistakable shaven dome. He's never able to admit as much within the show, but those four words tell us much about his inner psyche. If the game is no longer to provide for his family (which it wasn't after Season 1), then the game now is to have every last person bow down to the almighty power of his intellect. Walter White can say that he wants to be king. He can't voice that he wants to be God. Even though Walter may in fact live up to his given name, he still feels the need to call himself by another name, a more mysterious name, in order to assert himself in the business of making meth. You know this name.

He's the one who knocks.

Like a snug pork pie hat, hiding beneath the "Heisenberg" name fits Walter on every side. In a telling similarity, the real Heisenberg won the Nobel Prize in Physics in 1932 for his work in quantum mechanics. As you may recall, Walter once contributed research to a team that eventually won the Nobel Prize in Chemistry, as evidenced by a prized plaque in his house briefly seen in the pilot episode. Walter's endless need for respect even filters into his choice of a rather ridiculous alias for himself. If he can't retain the respect of his professional peers in the scientific world, he's going to do as much as he can to earn the respect of his peers in the drug world. In time, Heisenberg becomes a mysterious, fearsome name, known for a high-quality product and a low tolerance for disobedience.

In ways reminiscent of *Dr. Jekyll and Mr. Hyde* or *Fight Club*, Walter becomes Heisenberg, even when he doesn't have to be Heisenberg. Bryan Cranston said as much. "I wanted to create a sensibility that as long as he didn't recognize the man in the mirror, he could almost justify his actions. Like Jekyll and Hyde."[15] Though we're given a literal front-row seat to his devolution throughout the series, Walter's total transformation into Heisenberg most notably occurs when he decides to continue shaving his head despite his cancer's remission. This is a not-so-subtle wink-and-a-nod from the series' creators to let us know that, more often than not, Heisenberg is the man in charge of Walter White.[16] "There was a moment nobody ever really wrote about in the first or second season . . . when he was in remission from his cancer and he decided even though his hair was growing back, he decided to shave his head some more. And that was big thing for me because it made a statement that he was truly accepting this new life of his."[17] Cranston also related a subtle visual cue for Walter's full metamorphosis into Heisenberg: "We didn't have Walt stand erect until he became Heisenberg."[18]

Walter adroitly adopts a mystical moniker from the 20th century German theoretical physicist Werner Heisenberg, known most for his discovery of the uncertainty principle: "The more precisely the position is determined, the less precisely the momentum is known in this instant, and vice versa."[19] Though a complex notion, this is the uncertainty principle in its simplest form, defined by the original Heisenberg in 1927. As a way of understanding *Breaking Bad*, it's a key to Walter White's errant beliefs about himself. Through a vastly superior intellect when compared to those around him, Walter can precisely determine his position in any situation and plan for most contingencies. However, Walter is blind to the momentum—the consequences —of his actions.

Contrarily, if he knew the momentum of his actions, if he could see how every last one of his reprehensible choices could lead to his family's demise, he would (we hope) alter his course accordingly. Sadly, according to his eponymous physicist predecessor, you can only know position or momentum; it's impossible to know both simultaneously. Walter chooses to know his position at every turn, ensuring that he stays in control of his world at all times, ignorant of his increasingly deadly momentum.

To sum, the physicist Heisenberg decried causality in nature, that is, that every action has a predictable outcome if all the data about the action is known beforehand. Ironically, this is the mental world that our drug-dealing Heisenberg inhabits. He believes he can tell the future by rightly assessing every fact of the present. Throughout a vast majority of the series, Walter has been (mostly) right, but the audience knows that Heisenberg's hubris will eventually expose his weakness. In other words, the uncertainty that has directly resulted from his diabolical actions will find him. More specifically, the uncertainty principle will find Heisenberg's brother-in-law sitting on a toilet, thumbing through a used copy of Walt Whitman's *Leaves of Grass*.

"YEAH SCIENCE!"

Smalltime drug dealer Jesse "Cap'n Cook" Pinkman literally falls into the world of *Breaking Bad*, tumbling out of a second-story window clad in little more than his underwear. From the outset of the show, both Jesse and his would-be mentor share the shame of an ignominious and barely naked debut. Before Walter's even made his plaintive plea to his former student, the writers have provided us with a visual gag that instantly ties their central characters together. Could such parallelism in their introductions mean that these men will eventually be laid bare to the world? Or is it is a physical sign of their beginning innocence, "naked I came from my mother's womb?"[20] Or is it just a comedic introduction for two characters who will soon be consumed by serious issues? I'd guess the latter, but it's intriguing that *Breaking Bad*'s central characters are similarly presented in their on-screen debuts.

Echoing Mr. White and Mr. Pink from Tarantino's *Reservoir Dogs*, Walter White and Jesse Pinkman become the dastardly, drug-dealing duo of the ABQ. As evidenced by their last names and the show's unsurpassed cinematography, color plays an integral role in the world of *Breaking Bad*, an important aspect of the show that will be considered in the next chapter. For the moment, let's consider Jesse's unique surname.

As a Pinkman, Jesse's name evokes an equal shading of red and white, an amalgamation of innocence and guilt. As fans of the show know, Gale's blood stains Jesse's hands. Though manipulated to kill Walter's would-be replacement, Jesse is clearly revolted by his murderous actions as evidenced by his relapse and subsequent attendance at a Narcotics Anonymous meeting. His brutally honest admission of guilt at such a meeting in Season 4, Episode 7's "Problem Dog" is one of the most emotionally charged moments of that season and possibly of the series. Though couched in terms of shooting a "problem dog," Jesse is visibly unnerved by his own ease in regards to taking the life of another human. It is this remorse that makes Jesse "pink." He knows better than to think himself pure like Walter White. Eventually, he understands that he's done something intrinsically evil.

Interestingly enough, the name Jesse means "God's gift" or "God exists." While Jesse might believe himself to be God's gift to the ladies in his life, what if Gilligan is trying to tell us something more about Jesse's role in the *Breaking Bad* universe? We know that Walter White is breaking bad, falling from suburban status-quo to drug kingpin, tallying a body count only rivaled by the world's major dictators. Yet Jesse, the presumed idiot child and constant screwup, may be *breaking good*. Despite the hundreds of drastic and diabolical actions he's taken over the course of the show, most of which were instigated by Walter the puppet master, Jesse's morality appears to be forming into something much more wholesome than when we first saw him fall out of a second story window after sleeping with some guy's wife.

If Jesse means that "God exists," will Jesse's bent toward breaking good be the main catalyst for Walter White's inevitable downfall? Will Jesse turn on his former teacher and current mentor once he discovers the depraved depths that Walter White has descended to? When Jesse learns that Walter poisoned his girlfriend's son Brock with the Lily of the Valley (another biblical allusion), will his sense of moral rightness finally overcome his sense of loyalty? Will Jesse be "God's gift" to Walter's family, a sacrificial lamb that will save them, knowing full well he'll have to die to do so? The most notable Jesse, after all, was the father of David in the Bible, whose lineage eventually led to the birth of Jesus.

If "God's gift" is a "Pink Man," might he be a pure man washed in the blood?

"UNCLE HANK IS GOING TO BE A HERO!"

Aside from his vast collection of ~~rocks~~ minerals, we know Hank Schrader as a hard-boiled bulldog of a DEA agent. Resilient, persistent, and unswervingly devoted to justice, Hank pursues Heisenberg even when he's no longer assigned to the case. However, the writers offer us a real-life glimpse into the challenges of the drug war, showing Hank's marriage difficulties and his struggle with PTSD following Tortuga's explosion.

"Schrader" stems from the German professional title for "tailor."[21] Hank is the nickname version for Henry, and some sources relate that Hank is also related to the name John.[22] Henry stems from the German "haim" for home and "ric" for ruler, allowing us to know what we've already seen: Hank rules his home. Though he doesn't rule with an iron fist, Hank's mastery of his home and professional domains appears unrivaled, at least to his peers. However, we're witnesses to his fears and panic attacks, signs that even the indomitable and seemingly undefeatable Hank Schrader doesn't have complete control over his life. As we well know, the notions of power and control run like an escaping RV throughout the series. Still, Hank powers through his issues, relentless in his pursuit of the mysterious and dangerous Heisenberg.

Although I posited that Jesse may be the ultimate moral center of *Breaking Bad*, Hank may also be considered a possible Christ figure in this fascinating, unfolding drama. Consider this: with his body, Hank paid the price for Walter's actions. The Cousins from Mexico, thinking Schrader responsible for Tuco's death, stalk him throughout Season 3. If you recall, Walter attempted to kill Tuco in Season 2, Episode 2's "Grilled." Though Walter's ricin-laden taco plot was negated by a ringing bell of accusation from Hector "Tio" Salamanca, Jesse, in self-defense, eventually kills Tuco with a well-placed ~~mineral~~ rock to the temple. Hank comes upon the scene just as Walter and Jesse have fled, gets into a shootout with the wounded Tuco, then puts Tuco down for good. The Cousins know this and hunt Hank down in Season 3, Episode 7's, "One Minute." In the parking lot shootout, Hank kills one of the cousins and mortally wounds the other. However, Hank suffers a severe wound that nearly paralyzes him.

Though Hank doesn't know the extent of his brother-in-law's involvement in this life-changing event, it was Walter's plan all along to kill Tuco. Consequently, The Cousins should have been hunting Walter, and it is Walter who should have suffered such a grave punishment for his misdeeds. This theme replays itself over and over throughout *Breaking Bad*, where Walter White's actions and intentions eventually lead to catastrophic events affecting those he purportedly holds most dear.

It's the Heisenberg uncertainty principle at play: Walter's careful calculations to assert his own place in the world result in an unknown momentum that carries consequences far beyond his intentions. It's for this reason I believe the wrath that Walter's wrought is barreling toward his unsuspecting family. In the end, he will be forced to choose his legacy: his empire or his family. Since we've been warned that Walter will become Scarface by series' end, I fear for the White family's safety.

I also fear that Hank will once again suffer the consequences of Walter's actions in order to save his own family members, especially Walt Jr. and Holly, both of whom stayed with the Schraders in Season 5 as Walter and Skyler's marriage began to publicly unravel.

In the meantime, Hank could also be considered a Christ figure in that he is ever vigilant for justice. Hank wants to see the wrongs of the world righted. Though he may have a bull-headed way of getting that done, Hank ultimately desires to see the menace of meth erased from his hometown's streets. Although one could argue that bringing down Heisenberg may have more to do with showing off his accomplishments at his job or getting revenge on the man responsible for so much grief in his own life, we have to admire Hank's dogged determination. We see a man hell-bent on bringing at least a little bit of heaven back to earth.

In Hank Schrader we see a man fascinated with gems who has become a veritable rock himself, the only immoveable object capable of blocking the unstoppable force that is Walter White. Hank is the only man willing to stand between evil and good, hopeful that evil will turn from its ways, but well-prepared to ensure that such evil isn't allowed to harm one more person. If necessary, Hank will seek out his own full measures and pull the trigger on his brother-in-law without hesitation.[23]

"IT'S ALL GOOD MAN!"

When Saul Goodman burst onto the *Breaking Bad* scene in Season 2, the audience found a new character they could hate to love or love to hate. Bob Odenkirk's tacky suit portrayal of a small-time lawyer playing a big-time game outside of most of the laws of his state instantly won over the audience. In fact, the consistent popularity of the smart, smarmy lawyer resulted in a Saul Goodman spinoff.[24]

Formerly Saul McGill, Goodman purposefully changed his last name to something he thinks more palatable to possible clients, echoing the phrase, "It's all good man." To be blunt, Saul is anything but good. Knowledgeable about legal loopholes and adept at evading capture (both by the law and his own clients), Saul provides an ample amount of comic relief while simultaneously indicting America's litigious ways.

Like Tom Hagen in *The Godfather*, Walter and Jesse's new consigliere becomes a trusted advisor in the affairs of their business. With connections to a number of other ne'er-do-wells in the ABQ, Saul becomes an important part of the tight plot lines of the show. For instance, it's due to Saul's involvement with Walter and Jesse that they're eventually introduced to the quiet yet menacing Gustavo Fring. Goodman also "helps" them by placing "clean-up" guy Mike Ehrmantraut on their trail.

In history, Saul was the first king of the Jews. Various sources define the meaning of the name Saul as "asked for" or "prayed for." This is a fitting name for a character of whom much is asked of in times of need. Throughout the show, it's Saul's suspect legal intellect that helps Walter and Jesse evade certain capture. As one who is constantly asked for, Saul may represent the notion of prayer. When the stakes are highest and punishment is nigh, "Better Call Saul!"[25]

The name Saul also connotes the New Testament Saul, who, after seeing Christ on the road to Damascus, was rechristened Paul. Before becoming the author of most of the New Testament and the first major defender of Christianity, Saul killed Christians. While I doubt that *Breaking Bad's* Saul is headed for any kind of great awakening of conscience, might he undergo a change of heart in order to protect Jesse, or Walter's family, from Walter himself? Though Walter believes himself in power over Saul, Saul's knowledge of Walter's empire and underhanded actions provides Saul with a certain amount of leverage. Though Saul has been seen as a mostly powerless character who bends to the whims of his clients, might he have a road to Damascus moment at some point in the final eight episodes? Might he finally see the horror that his hands have helped wrought? Might Saul refuse even more money in order to save the lives of people he's grown to appreciate?

"Don't you want to see your daughter grow up?"

Fittingly, Skyler's name is said to be of Danish origin and can mean "fugitive or giving shelter." As a somewhat willing accomplice to her husband's new profession as a drug dealer, Skyler both provides shelter *and* becomes a fugitive. Though she was a lone voice of reason for a time, she eventually caved to Walter's whims as a way to protect herself and her family. After this turn of events, my thoughts echo Vince Gilligan's: "I like Skyler a little less now that she's succumbed to Walt's machinations, but in the early days she was the voice of morality on the show."[26] Her name obviously evokes the sky as well, another not-so-subtle nod that Walter lives in a world saturated by blue.

In Season 2, Episode 4's "Down," Walt Jr. demands to be called Flynn, ostensibly because he's ashamed to carry the same name as his father who's just suffered an embarrassing "fugue state" mental breakdown.[27] R.J. Mitte, the actor who portrays Walt Jr., asked Gilligan about the origin of the name Flynn, "out of all the nicknames." Gilligan's choice for Walt Jr.'s unique nickname was inspired by movie star Errol Flynn.[28] The phrase "in like Flynn" reportedly began as a result of Errol Flynn's womanizing ways, meaning that anyone who was "in like Flynn" was quickly accepted. It's not a stretch to think that

Walt Jr., a presumed outsider due to circumstance, would want to be "in like Flynn" in every sphere of his life. It's also ironic that Walt Jr. wants to distance himself from his father by giving himself a nickname when Walt Jr. is actually and perfectly emulating his father, who's also given himself a ridiculous nickname.

In regards to Walter's youngest child, baby Holly, her name evokes life, like the green branches of the holly plant. Intriguingly, holly is often seen around Christmastime, a symbolic plant in the Christian tradition. However, such associations are a coincidental stretch, as Vince Gilligan chose the name in honor of his girlfriend Holly, stating that he tries "to put her name or an allusion to some element about her into all of the scripts."[29]

Lastly, Mike Ehrmantraut's unique German last name perfectly describes him. "Ehr" and "man" equate to "man of honor," a questionable moniker given Mike's profession, but we know his loyalty to his employer is without equal, even if that employer requests highly illegal activities. "Traut" stems from the Middle High German trûen or trûwen, meaning to believe, trust, or hope, an ironic assessment of Mike who was ultimately betrayed for his trust in Walter White, despite Mike calling Walter a ticking time bomb and having "no intention of being around for the boom."[30]

WHAT'S IN A NAME?

Why focus on names? In addition to providing interesting insight into these characters, names have the ability to define us and redefine us. Throughout the Bible, a person's name reflects who they are. Quite often, a person receives a new name that provides guidance toward their future. For instance, Abram, the patriarch of Jews, Muslims, and Christians, receives the new name Abraham, meaning "Father of Many Nations."[31] His new name constantly reminds him that God would provide an heir to him despite his and his wife's advanced age. Later in the Old Testament, Jacob is rechristened Israel, meaning "God contends" or "prevails with God."[32] This is a reminder of the time Israel fought an angel of the Lord and asked to be blessed by God for his all-night-long struggle. Israel would go on to father twelve sons who would then beget the twelve nations of Israel.

Going forward a few millennia, Jesus changes Simon's name to Peter, meaning "rock," telling Peter that he would establish his church on such a rock. Peter would go on to become the first leader of the Christian church. Though a coward at Jesus' death, Peter becomes one of the staunchest of advocates for the gospel, one who, according to church history, eventually suffers the same type of death by crucifixion as Jesus. However, Peter considers himself unworthy to die in such a similar fashion and requests to be hung upside down.

Lastly, in one of the most shocking events of the New Testament, Saul becomes Paul.[33] Saul was among the first to persecute and kill Christians for their heretical beliefs. On the famed road to Damascus, Saul is struck blind during an encounter with the risen Jesus. He's converted on the spot and eventually begins to refer to himself as Paul following his conversion. The only time he talks about himself as Saul is when he's recounting his pre-conversion days. Some believe this was due to the name Saul being tarnished by the ancient

Israelite king Saul, a mad king who eventually became quite arrogant in his ways. In contrast, "Paul" means "humble," and this may have been a way for Paul to remind himself to stay humble despite his own arrogant and persecuting past.[34]

Though you may have been named after a family member or a fictional character, your name defines you.[35] Though you may be unaware of what your name literally means, you know what your name means to you. You have a basic understanding of what your name means to those you love. Your name carries weight. It either reminds you of who you are or encourages you toward who you're supposed to be. It may be a point of pride or a summons to shame. The weight of your name may be something you think about every day, or it may be something you've never thought twice about.

Regardless, God offers a new name to those willing to accept it. In the last book of the Bible, God says, "I will also give that person a white stone with a new name written on it, known only to the one who receives it."[36] In other words, there is a great book of life with all of our names written in it, but there are also millions of stones with new names inscribed upon them.

This is a promise from God that full redemption is always possible, that even the names we were born with, the names we sometimes shudder to live by, the names we're sometimes far too proud of or all too ashamed of, will also be redeemed. It's a promise that even the most basic part of our existence will be redeemed in the end. This new name is likely one that wouldn't make sense to us now, but will make complete sense only after our life on earth is done and our actions, motivations, loves, hates, desires, and hopes can be seen in full, from the vantage point of a God who knows us inside and out. Then and only then will we receive our new name, and it will fit us like no nickname we've ever received. That single name will perfectly define us.

If the media exposes Walter's double life, he's likely to receive a new, newsworthy name. If Jesse or Hank sacrifice themselves in order to stop Walter, they'll likewise receive new, laudatory names. Maybe no new names will arise by series' end, but it would be intriguing if our favorite characters in *Breaking Bad* receive new titles before it's all over, a telling sign that an irrefutable inner change has occurred.

They would all do well, as would we, to heed the words of Proverbs 22:1: "A good name is more desirable than great riches; to be esteemed is better than silver or gold."

"Blue, yellow, pink, whatever man."

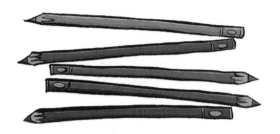

COLOR ME BAD

MICHAEL SLOVIS' AWARD-winning cinematography bathes *Breaking Bad* in gorgeous light and vibrant color. His beautifully framed shots of the New Mexico desert ensure that Albuquerque plays as much a role in the story as do its central characters. More intriguingly, his artfully composed scenes allow the simple aspect of color to play an integral role in the series.

Gilligan and Slovis knew exactly what they were doing. "Color is important on *Breaking Bad*; we always try to think in terms of it. We always try to think of the color that a character is dressed in, in the sense that it represents on some level their state of mind."[37] For instance, the pilot episode shows chemistry teacher Walter White wearing beige, a color he proceeds to wear less and less as the series continues.[38] Additionally, Walter's beige Pontiac Aztec isn't actually offered in such a color in the real world.[39] This hearkens back to Gilligan's stated intentions to make Walter someone who falls into the background of life, an average joe living an average life, that high school teacher whose name you can't quite recall. "Everything makes him blend into the walls."[40]

In a fascinating insight, writer Erin Enberg points out that Walter uses a red, green, and blue spray bottle in the pilot episode in order to create a flame from a bunsen burner. She views this simple act as a symbolic introduction to the quickly changing world of Walter White. When money (green), meth (blue), and death (red) collide, they produce a visible and violent reaction, uncontainable the longer it's allowed to exist.[41]

Obviously enough, one of the central colors within the *Breaking Bad* world is blue, the color of the pure crystal meth Walter produces.[42] While that color blatantly symbolizes Walter's descent into becoming a meth kingpin, Gilligan and company use the color to signify multiple, concurrent issues going on in Walter White's life. In Season 2, the city remembers those killed in the catastrophic mid-air collision above their town with blue ribbons, an everywhere-haunting reminder to Walter of his complicity in that tragedy.

When asked about the recurrence of the color blue in Season 3, Gilligan says that Walt does wear more blue that season, which to him is a "subtle indication of Walt moving towards Skyler," who's often seen wearing blue herself. However, if Walter's color palette shows his movement back toward his wife, what does her changing palette from blues to blacks and greens say about her movement toward her husband?[43]

When Skyler White attempts to kill herself by walking into their backyard pool in Season 5, Episode 4's "Fifty-One," she's wearing a blue skirt and becomes engulfed in a blue world. In other words, "her life is being consumed by Walt's involvement in the meth manufacturing business."[44] Even Skyler's name evokes the sky, a blue world that turns dark at least half the time. In "Gliding Over All," Season 5's midpoint cliffhanger episode, Skyler and Walter visit a storage unit containing their stacks of yet-to-be laundered cash. Skyler and Walter both wear blue, a subtle visual cue linking them together, complicit as they both are in Walter's empire-building.

It may go without recognition because of Walter's bland surname, but white reveals itself to be a distrustful color. White is, of course, Walter's last name, and we know Walter to be an impure soul despite his protestations to the contrary. Normal crystal meth, i.e. that which Walter deems inferior, covers a range of white tones. It can be clear or milky white, a substance that looks innocent enough, but wields an evil addiction within its otherwise translucent exterior.

On the other hand, white represents a certain purity, or a step toward repentance. Jesse paints his graffitied room white after images of Gale's murder haunt him. It's an external sign of an internal battle. Still, Jesse wears both black and white as he later recounts the murder under the guise of wantonly killing a "problem dog." Throughout the show, the yin and yang of white and black constantly battle each other.

For such a violent show, it's fitting that red plays a constant and terrifying role in the series. The meth lab rebounds with red, a visual precursor to the heartless horrors that occur in Season 4, Episode 1's "Box Cutter." Gus Fring dons a red jumpsuit to keep his business clothes clean and coldly murders his henchman Victor as a warning sign to Walter and Jesse.

They are stunned by the unexpected turn of events and their boss's blatant, terrifying disregard for human life.

Like the fear that any *Star Trek* fan has when a character dons a red shirt, seeing red on *Breaking Bad* leaves the viewer with the uneasy anticipation that something very, very bad is about to occur. Jesse wears red when he kills Gale. In "Gliding Over All," the local news anchor wears red as she reports on the (Walter-orchestrated) deaths of nine inmates and one lawyer. The tarp that the White's astounding piles of cash sit upon is red, which could either be a symbol that this cash was earned on top of the blood of hundreds of individuals, or a sign that the Whites will pay dearly for the sins they've committed in their pursuit of wealth.

Lastly, of the more important colors on the show, green represents money, of course, but it could also be considered to represent life. As one commenter on AMC's website put it, "As the show progresses so does the color of [Walt's] clothes from the color green to a gradual descent to black as he descends into darkness . . . the color green symbolized life for him and his go-ahead in pursuit for money. Green is the color of life and that's what he's after, away from his milquetoast life and a desire for control."[45]

I'd argue that green always and ever symbolizes Walter's quest for more money, as that seems to be one of his main motivating factors for what he does, his main justification for all of the atrocities he commits in the name of "providing for my family."

Yet other smart viewers see living greenery as a stark contrast to Walter's bent toward murder. In describing the riveting and tragic death of Mike Ehrmantraut, one reviewer said of Mike, "He went out, at least, among the bright plant life of the trees and brush by the river where he skipped his last stones, an exceedingly rare sign of life (and a color that's almost never used in the series) in the blasted landscape that is Walt's domain."[46]

For a series that mostly occurs in the desert, to show dense foliage along a river bank is visually shocking. It's a quiet, peaceful scene bursting with life, but drowning in desperation.

BACK IN BLACK / PURPLE HAZE

In regards to the secondary color palette of *Breaking Bad*, consider the show's usage of black, gray, yellow, pink, and purple.

As the show progresses, Walter's general attire evolves from beige to green to black, especially as his inner Heisenberg becomes his outer persona. In some ways, he becomes the man he wanted to be years ago. When Walter and his graduate school friend Elliot Schwartz started Gray Matter Technologies, they devised the name as a play on their own surnames: White plus Schwartz (German for "black") makes gray. However, due to undisclosed reasons, Walter sold his part of the company for $5,000. Schwartz would later marry Gretchen, a woman with whom Walter once enjoyed a close working relationship, a relationship that was likely intimate at some point.

After Walter's departure, Gray Matter Technologies would go on to earn billions of dollars and win a Nobel Prize, mostly due to work based on Walter's ideas. In addition to his black clothes representing his descent into darkness, Walter may subconsciously be attempting to become like Schwartz, the man whom he sees as having stolen the best years of his life, the money due his intelligence, and the academic peer of a wife he once only daydreamed about. Prolonged vengeance slowly turns a dark heart inside out, so it should come as no surprise that Walter White turns to black attire.

Walter and Jesse's utterly recognizable yellow HazMat suits denote danger, the same way a yellow warning sign screams "stay away!" Used while cooking meth in their Fring-owned meth lab, the suits call careful attention to the fact that their job is highly dangerous. A false move, a missed step, or an errant calculation could result in an epic explosion. The same could be said for the greater narrative of *Breaking Bad*. Walter and Jesse's world could implode at any moment if either of them makes a false move, misses a step to cover up their actions, or underestimates their foes.[47] That they wear yellow so often suggests that *both of them* are the danger.

Consider too that the primary colors of *Los Pollos Hermanos* and Gus Fring's wardrobe choices are both heavy into yellow. The ridiculous fumigation tents that Vamonos Pest Control uses are yellow and green, possibly a wink and a nod to the fact that the tarps are used to hide Walter and Jesse's highly hazardous, money-making business.

In addition to the pink literally included in Jesse's last name, the color itself makes its most notable appearance in the Season 2 opening episode, "Seven Thirty-Seven." In the very first scene, a one-eyed, pink teddy bear with half its face charred floats in a pool. Shot in black and white, the only color on the screen is the bear's pink. Eventually, we discover that this bear fell into Walter's pool as a result of the midair collision of Wayfarer flight 515 and a Boeing 737.

Through one of the most brilliantly executed plots on TV, this accident occurred as a result of Walter's sins. Consequently, the color pink could symbolize innocence or judgment.[48] The floating pink teddy bear that haunts all of Season 2 makes a constant visual reference to the 167 people that died as a result of Walter's decision to let sleeping junkies lie.[49] It symbolizes the innocence of those who were wholly unaware of the significant series of events that occurred prior to their terrifying deaths. It also symbolizes the judgment that Walter faces for his sins. He's even wearing a pink sweater as he witnesses the collision above his home.[50]

In Season 4, Episode 4's "Bullet Points," the color pink is vocally referenced by *Breaking Bad*'s resident gemologist, the recuperating Hank Schrader. In showing his precious ~~rocks~~ minerals to Walt Jr., the erstwhile Flynn asks his uncle, "What makes it be all pink like that?" Hank replies, "Well, that's the Manganese part, OK? It oxidizes, like rust." Walt Sr., ever the teacher and ever the one to show his intellectual superiority, chimes in: "Exactly. Manganese can have an oxidation between minus three and plus seven, which takes it through a range of colors—purple, green, blue—but its most stable state is plus two . . . which is usually pale pink."

Astute *Breaking Bad* observer Erin Enberg notes how well this seemingly random bit of rocky conversation coincides with Walter and Jesse's relationship, the pale pink that's produced when White meets Pinkman. "When they're torn apart, either from fighting each other or having other people plot them against each other, things go very badly. But when they work together, their messed-up world is the most stable." Their most stable state is "plus two."[51]

Still, the most frightening and foreboding aspect of this particular color symbolism, one that can connote judgment, innocence, and death, is that little baby Holly's often seen safely ensconced in her pink blanket. Could this foreshadow a heartbreaking loss, an ultimate judgment on Walter's sins, by series' end?

On a lighter note, anyone who's seen at least a few episodes associates only one color with Marie Schrader: purple. In an interview with the AV Club, Betsy Brandt revealed how her character came to be so enamored with the color: "We were all assigned a color—mine was purple—and I said, 'Well if her color is purple, then I think she just loves purple. She is really, really into purple.' She's that kind of person. She doesn't do anything half-a—. And Vince said, 'Great!' And now everybody's color has changed except for mine. I'm like, 'How come everybody else's color is changing, and mine's not?' And [costume designer] Kathleen Detoro said, 'Vince likes you in purple.'"[52]

In other words, sometimes a color is just a style choice. Then again, the fact that "everybody's color has changed" reveals how much each character (aside from Marie, apparently) has evolved over the course of the series. It's not just Walter who's undergoing a drastic metamorphosis. The colors that the characters wear as the series progresses key us in to such a fact.

Knowing what you know now, after having watched the show and read this chapter, you can't help but to notice the unmistakable colors used in *Breaking Bad*. Without the use of voiceovers or other narrative tricks that would quickly take us out of the story, the creative use of color throughout the series tells us much about the inner worlds of these fascinating characters. In addition to the recognized talent of the cast as a whole, where a lingering look tells us much about their moral dilemmas, these colors provide a guideline for us to better assess the notable difference between a character's intentions and their actual actions. More often than not, these conflicted characters act their color, so to speak, rather than act on their words. It's as if Vince Gilligan and his creative team made his characters bare their inner motives in every scene, their clothes like starkly color-coded souls.

"Lung cancer. Inoperable."

A TICKING TIME BOMB OF DEATH

INCREDIBLY, WALTER WHITE carries the direct or indirect responsibility for the deaths of 268 people.[53] With 62 episodes, an average of 4.32 people die *per episode*.[54] While someone doesn't die in each episode, death pervades the series like air. Used as a weapon of justice, a reminder of the effects of terribly bad choices, or a chilling glimpse into Walter's worsening soul, death is just as much a character in the *Breaking Bad* universe

43

as is anyone else.

Experienced screenwriters point to "the ticking time bomb" as a surefire way to engage an audience from the very beginning of a show to its conclusion. Think of the clichéd image of the dastardly villain strapping his kidnapped vixen onto train tracks. As the audience sees and hears the oncoming roar of a train, their pulse quickens, their grips tighten, and their breath shortens. They're having a visceral reaction to the tension on screen. Like the ever-increasing scream of a boiling tea kettle, they know that something explosive is about to happen.

In that scenario, the expectation of death or salvation for the innocent victim enraptures the audience, holding their minds captive until resolution occurs. In almost every movie or TV show that manages to sustain an audience's attention while causing an emotional reaction, you'll find the ticking time bomb motif, though the bomb itself could take many different forms.

In *Breaking Bad*, the ticking time bomb has a long fuse, but it's lit in the very first episode.[55]

Following the astounding and disorienting opening sequence of the pilot episode, we flash back three weeks prior and see Walter White, family man, enjoying eggs for breakfast. Topped with veggie bacon in the shape of the numbers 5 and 0, we learn it's Walter's birthday. We surmise that Sklyer, his wife, rules the roost, subtly goading him about working too many hours. His son, Walter Jr. ambles into the dining room on crutches. He lives with cerebral palsy, as noted by his slow, slurred speech and distinct walk.[56] A slight cough from Walter Sr. subtly hints at the diagnosis he's soon to receive.

A few scenes later, Walter suffers a coughing fit and passes out while working his second job at a car wash. In the very next scene, we see Walter upside down on the screen in a top-down shot of him in an MRI machine, a subtle cinematic hint that Walter's world is likewise about to be turned on its head.

Then, *Breaking Bad* showcases one of the best dramatic portrayals of a life-altering moment I've ever seen on TV. Words turn into unheard mumbles, silence becomes a high-pitched squeal mixed with the hum of an air conditioner, and Walter searches for absolutely anything else to focus on aside from the brutal truth of the moment. As his doctor tells him he has inoperable lung cancer, Walter can only focus on the mustard stain on the doctor's jacket. However, Walter's smart enough to understand his doctor through the din of his own death sentence. "Best case scenario with chemo, I'll live maybe another couple of years . . . It's just that, you've got mustard . . . right there."[57]

In this short sequence, the writers have accomplished three very important tasks.

Through the incongruity of Walter's response to his doctor —I'm going to die, but your stain really bothers me—they've revealed that *Breaking Bad* will not solely revolve around the far-too-real-life issues of cancer, death, and drugs, but will break the serious tension in a darkly comedic way.

They've also set a major plot point in motion.[58] Namely, Walter's deteriorating health paves the way for his otherwise innocent soul to rationalize selling drugs in order to provide for his family. His death sentence allows him to mistakenly believe that what he intends to do is for the good of his family. His decisions throughout the show are a classic lesson in the end justifying the means. This is an important issue that lives just beneath the surface of the entire series. Characters constantly weigh the benefits of their actions, and Walter's actions and self-justifying ways are the most egregious of them all.

Lastly, and maybe most importantly, Walter's lung cancer lights the fuse of the ticking time bomb. He knows he's going to die. His immediate family eventually learns that he's going to die. But most beneficially to the show, we know he's going to die. In subsequent scenes to his diagnosis, Walter tells no one about his bad news. The viewers are the first ones privy to this news, and it is through this looming specter of death that the writers ingeniously weld Walter's well-being with our sympathies. Suddenly, we're very emotionally involved with this dying man, someone whom we just saw a few minutes ago in his underwear, pointing a gun at oncoming sirens.[59]

Vince Gilligan speaks to Walter's cancer as the show progresses.

Walt's cancer did kind of take a back seat this season [Season 3], which does not mean that it won't resurface at some point. Walt, in my mind, does indeed have cancer. And it is in remission right now, but remission, it should be noted, does not necessarily mean a total cure. We probably have not seen the last of Walt's cancer. But his current state of relative health is kind of an irony in itself. He got off on this whole tangent of becoming a criminal due to his realization that he didn't have long to live. And as we saw towards the end of Season 2, when Walt suddenly got some good news, he didn't quite know how to react. He had felt bitter and betrayed by his own body, and said 'The hell with it. I'm going to be a meth cook.' And now he may live for years to come and in the meantime he's sold his soul and become a bad guy. That is one of those ironies we love as writers.[60]

In addition to providing a glimpse into the fact that the writers have most definitely not forgotten about their ticking time bomb, Gilligan also reasserts Walter's justifications for his actions. He's going to die. In many ways, isn't this our often understated, even subconscious, motivation for many of the things we do in life? The surprising and terrifying nature of death prods us from the future to make the most of our present. While such morbid thoughts most often banish themselves from our minds for most of our days, death cannot be escaped. We don't want to share much in common with Walter White, but at our most basic, human level, we do, and the writers insist we understand our similarities so that our journey with Walter White begins with empathy.

Death is our common enemy.

DEATH IN THE GOSPELS

In *Surprised by Hope*, professor and theologian N.T. Wright neatly summarizes why thinking about death is proper, even beneficial. "From Plato to Hegel and beyond, some of the greatest philosophers declared that what you think about death, and life beyond it, is the key to thinking seriously about everything else—and, indeed, that it provides one of the main reasons for thinking seriously about anything at all."

And yet, how often do we truly and deeply consider our lives? How often do we try to assess our days in light of the fact that with every day that passes, we're one day closer to physical non-existence? Even right now, you know the answer, and it's one of the reasons we resonate with Walter White in the pilot episode.

Fear.

We fear death for all that it entails. No one knows for sure what lies behind that veil, or what dance our feet will do when we finally shuffle off of this mortal coil. No one knows how many more breaths they're granted, or whether they'll die in peace or in pain. Among the weighty questions that *Breaking Bad* makes us ask ourselves, the series begins with asking the weightiest of them all: What are you going to do now knowing that you are going to die?

During the writing of this book, news broke that famed actor James Gandolfini died of an apparent heart attack. You likely heard the news. Though appearing in many movies and TV shows, Gandolfini is most well-known for his inimitable role as Tony Soprano.[61] In addition to establishing HBO as a powerhouse of engaging, original content, *The Sopranos* also filmed one of the most talked about series' endings in recent history. As the last scene suddenly cut to black, many viewers wondered if something went awry with their TV sets. Keen audience members suggested Tony was killed and the series simply represented the abrupt nature of our release from earth.

Isn't it telling though that we'd rather believe something wasn't working correctly than to lend credence to the fact that death may have overtaken even the powerful Tony Soprano?[62] If we're honest with ourselves, we don't want death to take down our powerful figures because we think, "If it can get them, it will surely get me." We constantly and subconsciously bend to irrational hubris.

We seldom speak about death in polite circles unless someone close to us, or someone famous, has passed. As a popular figure, actors like Gandolfini become water-cooler talk for the next business day, as co-workers and friends reminisce about their favorite *Sopranos* scene. Yet a few days later, such reminiscing is quickly forgotten, and the next time we watch an episode of *The Sopranos*, someone will very likely ask, "Didn't he die?"

Unless in deep mourning over a close family member who has passed, we often treat death as a casual interloper in our lives. While a fine line lives between glorifying death and relegating it to non-existence through subconscious ignorance, our society could benefit from a healthier perspective about death, one that causes us to seriously pause our days in order to reassess our lives in light of the deaths that do touch us personally. In other words, what life changes did you make the last time someone close to you, or even someone in the news that you respected, passed?

In the Bible's New Testament, death dwells in the background of the gospels, making rare but powerful appearances. In the Christian tradition, one of the reasons God sent his son to the earth was to defeat death, to forever kill that which attempts to kill forever.

Within Christianity, death is not a character to be feared. Rather, death is portrayed as an adversary sure to be defeated. Famous 19th century preacher Charles Spurgeon said, "When the time comes for you to die, you need not be afraid, because death cannot separate you from God's love." The Apostle Paul, in his first letter to the Corinthian church, stated this bluntly when he wrote, "The last enemy to be destroyed is death."[63] In that same letter, Paul openly mocks death, proclaiming "Where, O death, is your victory? Where, O death, is your sting?"[64] Paul's assurance that death is not, in fact, the final chapter for humankind extends from his belief that Jesus' grisly death on a cross paved the way for humans to experience life after death. Since the price for our sin has been paid through his sacrifice, death is not the ultimate scene for those who believe that Jesus actually and completely defeated death. Consequently, Christians are taught not to fear death, but to see it as simply a transition into a final state of being.

While death may be a passageway to meet God, one could also argue that death grieves God because it was never his intention for humans to physically perish.[65] The story of the fall of mankind as recounted in the book of Genesis is a tragedy without equal, a narrative that still echoes itself in myriad ways through the stories we hear and watch today. Adam and Eve were given absolutely everything they could have imagined, and yet they chose *the one thing* off limits to them. As a result, their perfect communion with God became a relationship wrought with peril. Their freedom to choose led to their ability to die.

Ironically enough, the one thing Satan promised them, eternal life, was the one thing he sought to steal from them. Consequently, Christ worked to defeat death in order to right what once was wrong.[66] Since Christians believe that Jesus was pre-existent, we believe Jesus personally experienced the fall of man. Seeing how our poor choices betrayed his father's trust and love, it's not too assumptive to believe that Jesus' quest to conquer death was incredibly personal.

One of the most well-known Bible verses is known for its

brevity, but even its brevity conveys an immense amount of sorrow over the death of a friend. John 11:35 famously says that "Jesus wept," but do you know why? He'd just been told that his friend Lazarus had died. Jesus would quickly raise his friend from the dead, a miraculous sign of his power over death, yet what sense does it make for Jesus to weep if Jesus knew what he was about to do next? Jesus wept because he knew of the sorrow and heartache that death causes. He wept for his friends who'd lost their friend. He wept for the pain that Lazarus may have suffered. He wept for the plight of humanity, a death sentence we placed on ourselves, but that only he can lift. Though Christians aren't to fear death, properly and sincerely mourning the dead is something even Jesus did.

For many people today and for the fictional characters who inhabit the world of *Breaking Bad*, death is a constant character, a looming figure seldom acknowledged but ever-present in the background of every scene. He's heard in the muffled coughs of Walter White, felt in the cold glares of Gustavo Fring, and viscerally experienced in every shocking death that occurs on the show.

The fear of death propels a wide array of bad decisions within the *Breaking Bad* universe, many of which result in a death, a veritable cycle of destruction. The characters continually sacrifice others in place of themselves. There are multitudes of instances where one person has to die, whether it's because they know too much, are in too deep, or are a loose end that needs an ultimate tie-down.

- In the first season, Walter kills Krazy-8 because he knows Krazy-8 will kill him, as evidenced by a missing piece of a shattered plate.

• In Season 2, Walter allows Jesse's girlfriend Jane to die from an overdose. She's a loose end who stole his partner and urged Jesse to start using drugs again. Jane's death ultimately leads to the deaths of 167 people when Wayfarer 515 and JM 21 collide in mid-air over Albuquerque.

• At the end of the third season, Walter sends Jesse to kill Gale, the intelligent lab tech he knows will eventually take over his role as Gus Fring's meth producer.

• In Season 4, Salamanca explodes Gus. In one fell swoop, Walter claims his throne by having his two greatest enemies negate each other.

• The jailhouse bloodbath in Season 5 is especially chilling, the result of Walt's need to keep his actions secret.

• The ultimately unreasonable death of hitman Mike Erhmantraut reveals Walter's heightened paranoia as a new drug kingpin.[67]

• Hank Schrader and his right-hand man Steven "Gomy" Gomez pay the ultimate price for getting involved in the Heisenberg case.

Every death orchestrated by Walter's intellectual prowess is an *anti*-atoning sacrifice, where sin and depravity vault Walter's worth above anyone else's, so much so that taking a life so that he doesn't have to give his own becomes as frictionless as his lying. So long as Walter can prevent himself from dying or his immense house of cards from falling, everyone else around him is fair game to be shipped down the river Styx. Within the larger narrative, at his core Walter fears dying, and this fear causes him to do unspeakable things in the name of ego, honor, family, respect, and professional ambition.

Having cast off the moral restraints of a high school chemistry teacher, Walter White's depravity is most clearly seen in his blatant disregard for life. If a person in his world can't help him make money, cook meth, or hide his tracks, they're prone to be dead within a matter of weeks. Despite his intellectual protestations that he's still a good guy—witness his shockingly funny pros and cons list before killing Krazy-8— Walter cannot proclaim innocence when it comes to matters of morality. Though his hands appear clean, we know that every death in the show can be traced back to the ultimate puppet-master.

BREAKING SIN

When I watched the first season of *Breaking Bad*, I sat transfixed by this small, strange, intoxicating universe of characters and experiences I knew nothing about. Even though they inhabited a vastly different world, their motivations to do absolutely heinous things seemed all too familiar.

As the series progressed, I kept waiting for Walter's lies to catch him like a trap he'd forgotten he'd set. He'd inch ever closer to the precipice of being found out, only to be granted a reprieve through circumstances he orchestrated. Like any good, tense drama, someone or something always rescues Walter from getting found out. You'd think it would happen sooner or later given his brother-in-law is a DEA agent, but the show makes this cat-and-mouse game work; in fact, that's part of the show's allure. However, by Season 5, Episode 8's "Gliding Over All," we know that Walter's finally been made. He will be found out, and it will not go well for him.

Let's rewind to a seminal moment in Season 3. Walter's lies continue unabated. As the cost for being discovered escalates, so too do his over-the-top lies. At the end of Season 2, two commercial planes collide above Walter's hometown. Through a brilliantly written series of events, Walter's actions (or, more appropriately, inaction) led to this catastrophic event that kills 167 people. The air traffic controller responsible for the crash recently lost his daughter to a drug overdose. This daughter is Jesse's girlfriend. When Walter visits Jesse, he sees Jesse and Jane asleep in bed. Jane begins to choke, and Walter cooly allows her to gag on her own vomit. He quite purposefully allows her to die, then lies to Jesse about his (non)involvement. Her death is yet another escape for him. Had she lived, Walter would have surely been found out. At the very least, he would have lost his partner in crime.

Though this is a shocking plot point, it isn't surprising. Given Walter's history, and how ardently he's had to fight to keep his tower of cards from falling, this is inevitable. What was not inevitable, and what he never could have seen coming, were the reverberations of that one act. This had been a minor theme of the entire series, but now, in the epic collision of two planes leaving scattered body parts across his hometown, the motif is writ large as if in skywriting: Walter, your sins hurt everyone around you. In this instance, his sins resulted in literal fallout.

So color me shocked (and yet not) when, at the halfway point of the first episode of Season 3, the high school that Walter teaches at holds an all-school grief counseling meeting to air their feelings about the tragedy that physically and metaphorically rained down upon them. After a few students share, and one questions God's goodness (to which the principal replies, "Can we just keep it secular?"), Walter is prodded to say something. In front of hundreds of students suffering from a shared traumatic event, Walter rationalizes the plane crash. "Look on the bright side. Nobody on the ground was killed. Neither plane was full. What you're left with, casualty-wise, is just the fiftieth worst air disaster. We will move on and get past this, because that is what people do."

In reality, he's not talking to the gym full of students at all; he's talking to himself, attempting to assuage his own guilt.

This is what hiding sin makes people say. I know this because I've both seen and heard it from others as well as being its mouthpiece. Sin compares itself to worse things, or worse people. Sin builds upon itself because it has to, because great would be its fall if it fell. Sin speaks from a place of self-sustain instead of self-sacrifice. Sin focuses on what is out there and what is wrong with someone else instead of what is within and wrong with oneself.

Even in the face of insurmountable evidence, sin will lie. Sin lies because it knows of no alternative. Unless light breaks in and grace abounds to the chief of sinners, sin must justify itself over and over or else our minds would be left with the devastating thought that *I am a bad person*. Just think of the cliché of those in jail, most of whom proclaim their innocence despite evidence to the contrary. We all do this in some form or fashion, whether we acknowledge it or not.

But there's a way out of this sin cycle, a pathway toward a better tomorrow, yet it requires a brokenness toward humility that doesn't lend itself easily to one whose pride is central to their personality. For redemption to even be a possibility, the sin must be acknowledged by the one at fault and recognized for its evil grasp on the sinner and its devastation on those around them.

However, ramifications remain. People perish. Relationships lie in ruin. Physical, mental and spiritual scarring occur. If the truth ever does come to light, if responsibility is taken, shouldered by the one to blame, it's only the beginning of the journey and not its destination.

I had hope that Season 3 would signal Walter's new beginning, a coming-to-terms with his own diabolical ways. However, we know this was never supposed to occur, and Gilligan makes it blatantly clear at the end of the premiere episode of Season 3. In that season opener, Jesse returns from rehab, clean. He and Walter discuss the cataclysmic events that have unfolded around them.

Walter, in response to being questioned about the crash, continues to find a scapegoat and says, "Really, I blame the government." Jesse, with a newfound moral center, relays what he's been taught at rehab: "You either run from things, or face them, Mr. White. It's all about accepting who you really are. I accept who I am." Walter asks, "And who are you?" Jesse replies, "I'm the bad guy."

In the next scene, Walter visits Gustavo Fring, telling him he's out of the game, deliberately stating, "I am not a criminal." Fring offers him $3 million for three months of work. "You can't change my mind," Walter responds. The scene ends without resolution, yet we know Walter's answer since an entire season still remains to be played out.

Walter White will not accept the fact that he's the bad guy.

Jesse, at least, realizes his own woeful shortcomings, even attempting to unsuccessfully cut ties on repeated occasions with his life of crime. The only way that Jesse's even able to begin that journey is by an honest assessment of his life, a shocking glimpse into his own deceitful heart. Through rehab, Narcotics Anonymous, and his own relationships, Jesse slowly learns that the world has not caused his problems—he has.

This hearkens back to a time before TV, when a British newspaper once asked popular authors to answer the question, "What's wrong with the world?" Prolific Christian author G.K. Chesterton replied with the shortest letter of his life:

"Dear Sirs, I am. Sincerely yours, G.K. Chesterton."

For Whom the Bell Tolls

At the core of the show, Walter hopes that his superior intelligence can earn enough money to provide for his family long after his passing. With cancer's death sentence set firmly around his neck from the very outset of Season 1, Walter's fears for his family's future seem to abate as his devious plan to cook meth coalesces. This is how he can make an incredible amount of money in a short amount of time.

However, he begins this nefarious extracurricular activity without weighing the actual costs of his disastrous choices. Sure, his plan works for a time, but viewers know from very early on that Walter's sins will eventually catch up to and overtake him. Though it will take the entire series for this to occur, brutal and swift judgment heads straight toward Walter's front door, kicked in by his own brother-in-law, DEA agent Hank Schrader.

Walter mistakenly pins his future hopes on himself, a dying, power-hungry, hubristic teacher bent on proving to everyone that he's unrivaled in intelligence, unmatched in meth-making, and unable to ever be discovered. His egotistical ways are the motivating factor for a number of incredible circumstances that most often lead to someone's gruesome death.

But what if there exists a greater intelligence than Walter's? Though it would be hard to comprehend for Walter, especially if he ever came into contact with someone who could outsmart him, there's always someone in the world who's better than us at something. Within the show, Gus Fring came the closest to Walter's level of cool sensibility. Gus had to be brilliant in order to maintain two distinctly different lives. And, it could be argued that Walter even respected Gus for the way he was able to delicately balance such disparate personas. But, Walter knew that Gus' empire prevented him from ascending to the proverbial throne of the local drug business, so he killed Gus with a ringing bell and reveled in the fact that his superior intellect won the day.

However, a greater intelligence does exist. Some may call it the justice of the universe—echoing Gilligan's statement that he "can't not believe there's a hell"—and others would call it "God." Regardless of how you might view this intelligence, it's an unmistakable force at work in the world of *Breaking Bad*. How else do you explain the rather happenstance moment when Hank innocently picks up Gale's gift to Walter, a copy of *Leaves of Grass*, a note to "W.W." inscribed within its covers? Some force or being much greater than Walter works against him. Whether you believe that's chance, justice, or simply the methodical and intricate plotting of master screenwriters at work is for you to decide. The point I'm getting at is that Walter believes his actions effect change, but he fails to recognize one of the foundational tenets of science: every action has an equal an opposite reaction.

In the book of Proverbs in the Bible, the writer says that "there is a way that appears to be right, but in the end it leads to death."[68] We will all suffer such a closing scene, a final moment of judgment on our lives, the last reckoning of our souls with an intelligence greater than our own. In that moment, we will know in full what we only knew in part while on earth. We will see the error of our ways. We will know what path we thought was right, but was in reality our selfish desires guiding our way.

Throughout Walter's journey, he's always thought his path to be right because its ending point—providing for his family —allowed for any kind of necessary detour along the way. Unfortunately for Walter, as bodies pile up along these waypoints, his changing motivations and the series of unforeseeable events he's set into motion have hijacked his journey. He will never arrive at his desired destination, whether that's providing for his family or becoming the most fearsome drug-dealer in the U.S. His hubris and the justice of the *Breaking Bad* universe will prevent that.

Salamanca's bell may have been quieted forever, but it's still ringing from the great beyond, and it tolls for Walter White.

"Better call Saul!"

JUSTIFYING THE UNJUST

As THERE IS honor among thieves, so too is there honor among drug dealers. Though separated by clearly demarcated territories, drug dealers in the world of *Breaking Bad* abide by a certain code of ethics that, when breached, more often than not results in death and a sudden redrawing of boundaries. Like smalltime generals, they carefully plot their reach, bide their time while other factions war against each other, then pounce on their adversaries when a prime opportunity presents itself.

This is a lesson Walter stumbles into learning, but, as the series progresses and his sense of self increases to epic proportions, Walter becomes an incisive, forceful commander of his own small army. He becomes a master chess player, plotting revenge in silence, orchestrating events so dastardly that realizing what he's done makes the viewer ill at the very thought that any man could have such thoughts *and* carry through with those thoughts.

For instance, consider when Walter poisons Andrea's son Brock. Walter commits this heinous sin in order to force Jesse back into his own good graces by placing blame on Gus for Brock's near-death experience. The writers hide this insidious move from us for nearly an entire season, another long fuse lit early and exploded late. When Walter makes an impassioned plea to Jesse that Brock's precarious future resulted from Gus's evil schemes, Jesse fully believes Walter's retelling of events. If we're honest with ourselves, we were just as duped as Jesse. That's one of the reasons we personally felt so betrayed in Season 4's finale, "Face Off." It wasn't that Walter had just lied to Jesse to get his own way. We're used to that. We expect that. The lie is wholly believable, and considering that Jesse's looking for a scapegoat, someone to vent his rage against, he's an all-too-ready believer in what Walt's telling him. Our ire rises at the fact that we fell for Walter's lies as well.

As the camera pans to the Lily of the Valley plant in Walter's backyard in Season 4's final episode, our collective heart sinks, awestruck that it was Walter all along who plotted so deviously to poison a child in order to win back Jesse, his only friend and confidante at this point. Just when we think that Walter White can stoop no lower, he almost kills a child.[69] In conducting such a symphony of lies, Walter White provides further evidence of his masterful though devious command of his world.

Later, he reprises this chorus of control when he defeats the chess grandmaster of the drug trade, Gustavo Fring, by capitalizing on the fact that "my enemy's enemy is my friend."

Through a shrewd series of decisions, Walter goads Salamanca[70] into killing Gus Fring in a suicide mission. Now, not only has Walter threatened the life of a child, he's also used an old man as a suicide bomb in order to murder his boss.

THE REALITY DISTORTION FIELD

Walter is the great betrayer Judas, selling his soul for a few silver coins. According to one interpretation of the notable betrayal of Jesus, Judas thought a physical revolution was on the horizon, a time when his people would rise up against their Roman captors. When he saw that Jesus was quite different from the conquering Messiah he expected, he decided to play chess with the God-man. Hoping that Jesus' arrest would cause him to revolt, fight, and bring redemption to the people of Israel through bloodshed and vengeance, Judas kissed Jesus in the garden, sealing both of their fates. When Jesus willingly subjected himself to death, Judas couldn't handle such an unexpected turn of events and hanged himself.

We constantly see Walter unable to cope with the unexpected events wrought by his own hands. Consequently, he keeps attempting to mete out his own version of justice, which all too often takes the form of vengeance, as evidenced by his machinations in dealing with Jesse, Brock, Salamanca, and Fring.

In Walter's world, justice is what he says it is. By paying Saul Goodman ridiculous amounts of money, he's able to bend justice to his will, even to the point of having 10 inmates killed in order to protect his secrets in Season 5, Episode 8's "Gliding Over All." This is ultimate power. But, as Lord Acton famously put it, "Absolute power corrupts absolutely." From having such intimate access to Walter's life, we know this to be true. To his core, Walter is absolutely corrupt.

Similarly, Judas expected to wield absolute power through the miraculous, revolutionary power he saw and experienced through Jesus. Once he discovered that Jesus' plan did not align with his own, he could no longer carry the weight of his own lofty expectations. Instead, he chose a length of rope and a tree branch to carry that weight.

When our notions of justice fail to align with the reality of a situation, it's very easy to give up. Whether someone with absolute power wields their might over our otherwise innocent, just actions, or whether real justice trumps our deceitful actions, each situation may result in a refusal to comply with reality as it is. More often than not, we want *our* way, regardless of whether our way would be considered the right way by most people. We are selfish to a fault.

This is one of the reasons we resonate with Walter, one of the many reasons we can still root for Walter despite his nefarious actions. He is us, again and again, over and over. It's often shockingly too easy to see ourselves in his clouded blue eyes. When he asserts his will to bend justice to his whims, we silently yearn for that kind of control over our own lives. Sure, we wouldn't delve into the evil of plotting near-death for a child, but we would consider lying to our boss so as to raise our stature within the company. We wouldn't engage in a wholly illegal profession in order to make money (at least one hopes), but we might consider every possible avenue in order to not pay the full amount of taxes we may owe the government.

There's an old saying within the church that sin is sin is sin.

Ostensibly, it means that one person's sins are no worse than another's. Our lies are equal to Walter's murders in the sense that both actions separate a person from God.[71] While the earthly ramifications of such actions are vastly different, a traditional Christian viewpoint sees every sin as carrying the same damnable weight as every other sin. Songwriter Sufjan Stevens magnificently captures this notion in his quiet, terrifying song "John Wayne Gacy Jr." The bulk of the song describes the serial killer and rapist who was responsible for the murder of at least 33 boys and young men. Stevens' last lines turn the song around, pointing a condemning finger back at himself and issuing a very hard challenge to the listener: "And in my best behavior / I am really just like him / Look beneath the floorboards / For the secrets I have hid."

What I'm getting around to saying is that *it's all the same.* Though the real-world ramifications of Walter's actions are wholly different than what may occur to a person who cheats on their taxes, the inner motivation is similar. It's still one person attempting to stamp their notion of justice onto the world around them. While they may be able to assert their will for a time, eventually their time will come. They will be found out, and justice will roll over them like an unstoppable flood.

Don't believe me? The litany of real, fallen cultural heroes is long: Lance Armstrong, Ted Haggard, Tiger Woods, Michael Vick, Pete Rose, O.J. Simpson, Joe Paterno, Tonya Harding, etc. It's intriguing to note that many of these cultural icons belong to the world of sports, possibly the most popular "religion" in the United States. Often removed from "real" society, these cultural icons exist in a bubble of their own creation, surrounded by men and women too in awe of their considerable talents to say anything closely resembling "No" to them. Like Walter, these icons can easily look at their lives and think "I did this. My superior prowess in athletics or business has led me to this empire. If I can do this, I can do anything." Whether or not they admit as much to themselves is irrelevant. Once they believe the lie of their own grandiosity, it may already be too late for their soul. They will attempt to bend reality to their every whim, much like Armstrong chose to lie for years about his doping habits.

If you tell the lie long enough and loud enough, people will believe you. So it goes with Walter White, the best liar on television.

GRACE AND COSMIC KARMA

Let's recall Vince Gilligan's fascinating quote about his take on morality in this world: "I want to believe there's a heaven. But I can't not believe there's a hell." In other words, Gilligan wants to believe in an ordered universe that sets right the wrongs perpetrated within it. He wants to believe that justice will prevail. The grand story arc of *Breaking Bad* can be boiled down to the Old Testament notion of an eye for an eye.

If that's the truth, then what can possibly happen to Walter White to ensure that he pays the full penalty for all the devastation he's wrought? When Gilligan asserts that the final eight episodes will be "victorious" for Walter, how are we supposed to interpret that?[72] Will he actually get away with all of the murder he's committed in indirect ways? Or will he receive his full comeuppance? Will he be forced to pay the ultimate price—death—in order that justice might be served?

In the *Breaking Bad* universe, justice, for the time being, means what Walter wants it to mean. Because of his intellect, Walter stays one step ahead of the law. He's able to think through most, if not all, of the direct ramifications of his actions. He's also diabolically able to manipulate others to do his bidding so that his hands stay clean. Unfortunately for those around him, Walter's sense of justice results in a catastrophic game of *Survivor*, where getting kicked off the island actually means being forcibly removed from earth. In Walter's mind, if your reason for being doesn't help him in some way, you're more liability than asset, and Walter's quick to dispatch his liabilities with full measures.

On the other hand, Walter disregards the fact that real justice has been hunting him down since he began his life of crime. Egotistically believing in himself to be able to outwit, outplay and outlast his adversaries, Walter thinks he will always be able to win the day. As we well know by now, a misplaced paperback becomes the first loose thread that will unravel Walter's morally threadbare universe. His bloodhound of a brother-in-law now has the scent. Justice is coming, and hell's coming with him. Though speaking to a different issue, this quote from the actual Heisenberg seems fitting: "The first gulp from the glass of natural sciences will turn you into an atheist, but at the bottom of the glass God is waiting for you."

If Gilligan holds true to the fact that he "can't not believe there's a hell," the tumultuous final eight episodes will show how *Breaking Bad* ascribes to a belief that many feel to be true of our actual world: cosmic karma, that is, you get what you deserve.

Bono, frontman for U2 and sometimes mouthpiece for

Christianity, deftly compares the notions of karma and grace, even using a metaphor Walter White would appreciate:

> The thing that keeps me on my knees is the difference between Grace and Karma . . . . You see, at the center of all religions is the idea of Karma. You know, what you put out comes back to you: an eye for an eye, a tooth for a tooth, or in physics; in physical laws every action is met by an equal or an opposite one. It's clear to me that Karma is at the very heart of the universe. I'm absolutely sure of it. And yet, along comes this idea called Grace to upend all that 'as you reap, so you will sow' stuff. Grace defies reason and logic. Love interrupts, if you like, the consequences of your actions.[73]

One of the most challenging aspects of the God of Christianity is the seeming incompatibility of a just God and a loving God. The argument goes that each defining characteristic cancels the other out. If God is just, how can he be loving? The Old Testament could be argued to show a petulant God that desolates entire populations of people in order for his chosen ones to advance. How does that show love for all?

On the other hand, if God is loving, how can he be just? The New Testament provides ample examples of God's loving nature as evidenced in the life of Jesus. But if God is love, why would a perfect man have to die in such an atrocious way? How can we reconcile two of the foundational, defining characteristics of God?

As an aside, this is a dense topic, and one that has been

debated for centuries by those much more intelligent than me."[74] However, let's consider this issue for a moment.

If God is perfect and defines himself by the word love, it goes to reason that every action he undertakes is motivated by love, *even the actions that result in people being forever separated from him in hell.* This is an incredibly difficult teaching. It's rooted in our ability to choose, a defining characteristic of being a human and being granted the ability to love. We can choose to inch toward God, or we can choose to inch away.

Author Billy Coffey presents this notion well in a true-life story. While sitting in a diner waiting for his lunch, a mysterious stranger approaches him, asks him if he goes to church, and then asks if he thinks non-Christians will go to hell when they die. The stranger echoes what many people may think about the way God works:

> Christians say that God is love, but if you don't go along with the program then you get eternally punished. That doesn't sound like love to me, that just sounds hypocritical.

> I shrugged. 'Not really. I reckon God's spent—what, fifty years or so?—trying to get you to pay attention to Him. He's arranged circumstances, given you a glimpse of things you don't normally see or think about, even spoke to you. There's no telling how many chances you've gotten to say 'Hello' to God after He'd said the same to you. But you have a choice. That's how He made you. You can choose to listen or not, choose to believe or not, choose to accept or not. I take it that so far, it's been not. So if you spend your whole life telling God to stay as far away from you as

possible, He's gentleman enough to do just that when it's all over. So yes, I suppose if you keeled over right here right now, you'd go to hell. But it's not me who's gonna send you there, and it's not God either. It's you."[75]

Coffey presents hell as an arrogant man's final destination. If you can live knowing about God's love but without responding to it, he's kindly enough to leave you be. Even then, 2 Peter 3:9 describes God as utterly patient: "The Lord is not slow in keeping his promise, as some understand slowness. Instead he is patient with you, not wanting anyone to perish, but everyone to come to repentance."

The work of Christ on the cross was the work of justification, a big word that means a big thing. Some pastors define the word with a phonetically similar phrase, justified is "just-as-if-I'd" never sinned. The love and justice of God converge in the person of Jesus. Since God allows only the just to be in his presence, and yet humans can in no way attain such perfection on their own, God's love manifested in the life and sacrifice of Jesus Christ provided a way for errant humans to become justified beings. However, this justification doesn't happen with a simple nod of assent by a person, attesting to the fact of their own depravity. Rather, it begins with an intense inner awareness of the vast differences between a holy God and a selfish sinner. It begins with humility in the face of holiness. It begins with a recognition that none of our bad choices *and* none of our grand accomplishments in life could push us further away, or bring us closer in, to a relationship with God. When we lean in closely enough to the teachings of Christianity, we learn to understand this seeming contradiction.

Pastor Tim Keller describes this notion quite well (emphasis added):

> The gospel of justifying faith means that while Christians are, in themselves still sinful and sinning, yet in Christ, in God's sight, they are accepted and righteous. **So we can say that we are more wicked than we ever dared believe, but more loved and accepted in Christ than we ever dared hope—at the very same time**. This creates a radical new dynamic for personal growth. It means that the more you see your own flaws and sins, the more precious, electrifying, and amazing God's grace appears to you. But on the other hand, the more aware you are of God's grace and acceptance in Christ, the more able you are to drop your denials and self-defenses and admit the true dimensions and character of your sin.

In a world where justice exists and hell is real, love must also exist to counterbalance the effects of the law. Without love, justice would be unduly and excruciatingly punishing. There would be no hope for anyone, let alone those who've committed the most heinous of deeds. By the end of *Breaking Bad*, the notion of love will play an intricate and important role in its conclusion, either as a saving grace for Walter or his family, or a final motivation for justice to extract its ultimate payment from Walter.

"I am the one who knocks!"

HEISENBERG'S HELL-BENT HUBRIS

ONE OF THE main motivating factors for Walter's continually climbing aspirations to become a drug kingpin rests in his lack of power in every other sphere of his life. The pilot episode clearly reveals his lagging self-confidence in multiple instances. He's married to a dominating wife (who later cheats on him), teaches inattentive students, and works for a demanding boss at a second job. After his cancer diagnosis, Walter must also come to grips with the sobering fact that he has no power to stop death. Consequently, much of the show revolves around Walter's quest for ultimate power and control over his life, his relationships, his work, and his world.

Throughout the series, slights to Walter's pride earn increasingly disastrous results for the perpetrators of those insults. The pilot episode adroitly plants the seeds for such abrupt, corrupt actions to occur in later episodes, as we see Walter quickly plot a grotesquely scientific way to kill off Krazy-8 and his sidekick. His pride goes on display again when he refuses to take money from Elliott and Gretchen Schwartz for his cancer treatments, still bitter over the fact that Gray Matter Technologies reaped billions off of Walter's own ideas, or sullen that Gretchen married Elliott instead of Walter. Accepting that money would have negated Walter's need to sell meth, but it was an affront to his pride, so he refused the Schwartz's largesse.

Walter's coy words often reveal his arrogance as well. In Season 3, Episode 1's "No Mas," Walter picks up a duffel bag filled to the brim with drug money. Hank picks it up as well, reminding Walter that he's not supposed to be doing any heavy lifting. Hank asks, "What you got in there, cinder blocks?" Walter wryly replies, "Half a million in cash." Hank laughs. "That's the spirit." A similar though more chilling exchange between Walter and Hank memorably occurs in Season 4, Episode 4's "Bullet Points." Hank reads the inscription inside of Gale Boetticher's lab notes. "'To W. W. My star, my perfect silence.' W.W. I mean, who do you figure that is, you know? Woodrow Wilson? Willy Wonka? . . . Walter White?" This time it's Walter's turn to laugh. Putting his hands up in a defensive position, Walter simply says, "You got me."

Later, clean-up guy Mike Ehrmantraut calls out Walter's increased arrogance: "We had Fring, we had a lab, we had everything we needed, and it all ran like clockwork! You could have shut your mouth, cooked, and made as much money as you ever needed! It was perfect! But no! You just had to blow it up! You, and your pride and your ego! You just had to be the man! If you'd known your place, we'd all be fine right now!"

Most fittingly, the book that wields the power to bring down Walter White's empire contains within it Walt Whitman's most famous poem, "Song of Myself," an ode to ego. Its opening lines sing out, "I celebrate myself, / And what I assume you shall assume, / For every atom belonging to me as good belongs to you." As evidenced by "you" in that line, Whitman brings the reader into his celebration. Likewise, our favorite W.W. brings us into his world every Sunday night, asking us to revel in his own celebrations of self. In watching the show, we gratefully join in this celebration, a damning indictment of our own proclivities toward constantly choosing self over others. More than just being entertained, we discover a shocking point of connection with *Breaking Bad*'s broken protagonist. The power he wields is the power we want. The establishment of self over all is the type of world we'd honestly prefer to inhabit. We'd never admit as much, but that's one of the reasons why we enjoy Walter's world so much.

Breaking Bad showcases a man whose hubris exponentially expands with each new episode. While attaining immense power over his world through his superior intellect, Walter's pride swells into God-like proportions. Such epic pride makes

Walter a narcissist like few others on TV and a striking, contemporary depiction of Satan.

A Mirrored Road to Hell

The classical Greek mythological tale of Narcissus speaks to our self-obsessed culture. As the child of a river god and a nymph, Narcissus held prestige as the most beautiful hunter of his time. What's worse, he believed the hype. The aptly named Nemesis, the spirit of divine retribution, knew about Narcissus' prideful leanings and his mean-spirited actions toward Echo, a nymph who'd professed her love for Narcissus, but was quickly rebuffed.

Nemesis coaxed Narcissus toward a pool. Upon finally gazing on his own beautiful visage, though not recognizing it as his own, Narcissus' self-fixation bolted him to that spot, ultimately resulting in a lonely, suffering, slow death. Other versions of this too-relevant story result in Narcissus committing suicide.

As you may already know, we have this tragic tale to thank for the word *narcissist*, one who thinks only of themselves.

While current cultural figures run the gamut when it comes to narcissistic tendencies, it's impossible to know the true depths of their selfishness without having insider access to their daily lives. How have their actions affected their loved ones? Do all of their friends and co-workers feel as if they have to kowtow to that person's every whim or else suffer some great casualty? Reality TV viewers can easily make assumptions about the two-dimensional "real" characters they're watching, but it's much more difficult to make the same kind of assumptions of someone you barely know.[76]

But we know Walter White.

We've been granted full access to the life and times of Walter White, chem teacher, meth dealer, family man, drug kingpin. While his motivations begin nobly enough—I want to be able to support my family beyond my quickly pending death —they quickly turn sour. While he may still tell himself that he's performing certain actions (full measures, if you will) for the benefit of his family, we know he's lying. He's bending reality to meet his needs, even as these needs change over time.

In the first season, Walter begins by sincerely wanting to make money to provide for his family should his cancer overtake him within the year. In his "brilliant" mind, selling the finest meth is the fastest way to make the most amount of money. In the third season, Walter's pride begins to boil. Motivated by a need to be the best in his business, which failed to happen during his time with Gray Matter Technologies, Walter goes so far as to have his learned doppleganger, Gale Boetticher, killed. As Season 4 and 5 progress, Walter overdoses on his own pride, killing the two men who tried to hold him under their proverbial fingers. No longer does he only want to make money or to be the best in his business—he wants to be The Man. He wants nothing less than total control of his situation. He wants Hyde to kill Jekyll. He wants to attain full Heisenberg.

Walter White is Narcissus, amazed by his own ability, even as it slowly kills him without him even noticing. "He doesn't realize what he's become. He has no clue. He's so in it and is so subjected to it that he doesn't have a good mirror image of himself anymore. He can't see how he's changed."[77] By default, the central, self-focused nature of pride makes the prideful person blind to the world around them, and their pride is often the agent of their undoing. As the author of Proverbs said ages ago, "Pride goes before destruction, a haughty spirit before a fall."[78] Ironically, despite the prideful person's infatuation with themselves, they're just as blind to the actual state of their own souls.

> This is not a show about evil for evil's sake. Walt has behaved at times in what could be regarded as an evil fashion, but I don't think he's an evil man. He is an extremely self-deluded man. We always say in the writers' room, if Walter White has a true superpower, it's not his knowledge of chemistry or his intellect, it's his ability to lie to himself. He is the world's greatest liar. He could lie to the pope. He could lie to Mother Teresa. He certainly could lie to his family, and he can lie to himself, and he can make these lies stick. He can make himself believe, in the face of all contrary evidence, that he is still a good man. It really does feel to us like a natural progression down this road to hell, which was originally paved with good intentions.[79]

So long as a prideful person can keep their ruse from being found out, a tiring process that requires a nimble mind and an unyielding adherence to their own careful fabrications, they can continue to justify their actions to make themselves appear like a good person. C.S. Lewis aptly described the state of such an ego-driven soul: "When a man is getting better he understands more and more clearly the evil that is still left in him. When a man is getting worse he understands his own badness less and less."[80] Unless a sudden tragedy occurs in the last eight episodes to break through Walter's arrogant facade, he will never come to understand his own badness.

In fact, Walter even manages to distance himself from the badness he actually creates. Ensuring that his sins are traced back to those nearest him, Walter tries to salve his writhing soul by goading those nearest him to take out his dirty laundry. For instance, who kills Gale? Who kills Gus? Who takes care of the 10 would-be snitches in prison? Walter's hands are clean, though the puppet strings he controls drip with blood.[81]

As a through-and-through narcissist halfway through the series, Walter's thoughts solely revolve around his own world. Though he may slip orbit every now and then and consider how his actions may be affecting his family, he seldom does anything with that knowledge, even when the effects of his actions blatantly reveal his sins and hubris. Take, for instance, his speech about Wayfarer flight 515, one of the most inured, emotionally numb speeches of all time. In fact, the name "Narcissus" is believed to have stemmed from "narke," meaning "to sleep" or "numbness." Walter attempts to rationalize the deaths of hundreds of people by comparing the crash to more catastrophic collisions, noting that the crash "casualty-wise, is just the fiftieth worst air disaster."

If Walter White's been asleep for half the series, what happens when he wakes up to the destruction he's caused? Will it be too late for him to change its course? Will his family suffer on his behalf? Will he commit suicide as an act of desperate penance? Will he be forced to choose between the kingdom he's built and the family he set out to provide for? Most essentially, what will have to occur so that Walter will be able to pull himself away from admiring the mirrored visage of a man in a black pork pie hat?

An Infernal Paradise Lost

Since the dawn of time, the slithering serpent of Eden has undergone a multitude of cultural wardrobe changes. Yet, in every epoch the Great Deceiver hides in plain sight, whispers utterly convincing lies into our gullible ears, and patiently waits for us to make a hell of heaven. Despite awareness of his machinations, we have always been infatuated with this former Angel of Light. *Breaking Bad*'s Walter White is among the latest costumes donned by this charismatic creature of the underworld. But first, let's look at a brief history of Satan's literary and cultural personifications.

Should you need a reminder of classical Christian belief, Lucifer, a.k.a. The Morning Star, was an angel in heaven, serving the Lord like all good angels should. He was thought to have been one of the most beautiful angels, matchless in appearance, save for the one he'd been created to serve. With hubris and arrogance overtaking him like a nightmare, Lucifer launched an attack on God, an all-out war of the angel armies that eventually ends in his banishment to hell. Let it be noted here that, surprisingly to us humans, Lucifer isn't killed, but is allowed to live, albeit far separated from the paradisal life he once enjoyed.

Isaiah 14:12-15 can be interpreted as speaking to his mighty fall: "How you have fallen from heaven, morning star, son of the dawn! You have been cast down to the earth, you who once laid low the nations! You said in your heart, 'I will ascend to the heavens; I will raise my throne above the stars of God; I will sit enthroned on the mount of assembly, on the utmost heights of Mount Zaphon. I will ascend above the tops of the clouds; I will make myself like the Most High.' But you are brought down to the realm of the dead, to the depths of the pit." Jesus confirms such a series of events in Luke 10:18 when he tells 72 disciples that he "saw Satan fall like lightning from heaven."

The name "Lucifer" is typically used for Satan's pre-fall identity. After his excommunication to hell, he becomes known as Satan, a.k.a. "The Opposer" or "The Accuser." Though the epitome of all that is wrong with the world, popular literary works have performed an interesting makeover on the Great Deceiver throughout the centuries.

In Dante's *Inferno*, released in the 14th century, Satan sits trapped in a sheet of ice at the center of hell, his great beastly body half-buried in the original, frozen Fortress of Solitude. Eternally gnawing on the three great betrayers of Judas, Cassius, and Brutus, Satan's batwings flap in a furious and impossible attempt at escape. The cold wind he generates causes the ice to stay frozen, an absolutely brilliant depiction of the frivolous, cyclical, and self-defeating nature of evil. The circles of hell are said to have been created in the exact spot where Satan landed after being cast out of Heaven.

Intriguingly, Dante's Satan makes The Evil One seem less diabolical than former depictions. Though the chief of sinners, Satan is still placed in the realm of yet another sinner suffering for his actions. This was quite a departure for the accepted notions of Satan in Dante's time, although it's in direct opposition to how the Apostle Peter describes him in 1 Peter

5:8. "Your enemy the devil prowls around like a roaring lion looking for someone to devour." In other words, Satan is not trapped in Hell as in *The Inferno*, but is a very real and active presence in the world, making humanity the focal point of a spiritual Battle at Kruger.[82]

Dante's Satan is so powerless that we almost start to pity him. He must endure the most brutal of all punishments: isolation. Satan doesn't even speak to Dante when he enters the last circle of Hell. Like children told to sit quietly and think about what they've done, readers may even feel sympathy for Satan's suffering, lonely plight. Our anger subsides, our impatience relents, and our hearts may even soften. Did the medieval world react the same way to Dante's Satan?

300 years later, John Milton released *Paradise Lost*, the sequel Satan desperately needed to revamp his meek image into the menacing yet suave Evil One. Published in the 17th century, *Paradise Lost* became the de facto standard against which all great villains were compared. Covering the story of Lucifer's fall from heaven and his subsequent temptation of Adam and Eve in the Garden of Eden, *Paradise Lost* is a masterpiece of a poem. Originally 10 books containing more than 10,000 lines of poetry, Milton would eventually expand his work to be 12 books, following in the steps of Virgil's *Aeneid*. He would also go on to write a sequel, *Paradise Regained*, though it never experienced the same kind of popularity as its predecessor.

In seeking to "justify the ways of God to men," Milton sets out to capture the story of the fall. If we can better understand the diabolical workings of Satan and his minions, we might better understand why God works the way he does. But, in creating such a story, Milton inadvertently created the world's first anti-hero, Satan. As cool as James Bond, as introspective as Freud, and as diabolical as The Joker, this Satan oozes charisma to the point where we find ourselves slowly nodding our heads in assent to the details of his unfortunate life circumstances.

The epic poem begins soon after Satan's banishment. Using his skills of persuasion, he rallies his fallen followers to his cause: poisoning the inhabitants of the earth in order to exact his ultimate revenge on the one who cast him into hell.[83] He sets his cause into motion by tempting Adam and Eve to disobey God's one command, resulting in their expulsion from the paradise of Eden.

In likely his most famous line, Milton's Satan describes himself very succinctly when he says it's "better to reign in Hell than to serve in Heaven." This kind of selfish idiocy runs rampant through humanity, a direct result of the Fall of Man. At the heart of a refusal of the gospel is the inability to bow one's knee to one's creator. It is the belief that God does not know how to rule, or if he even cares to rule at all. It is the yearning to be in control of one's destiny. It is an eternal motif seen in *Breaking Bad*, felt in our own lives, and told since the birth of humanity.

In many ways, Satan appears as the central character of *Paradise Lost* due to his conniving and charisma. Like actors are prone to note when taking on the roles of villains, they get all the best lines. In *The Marriage of Heaven and Hell* William Blake wrote, "The reason Milton wrote in fetters when he wrote of Angels & God, and at liberty when of Devils & Hell, is because he was a true Poet and of the Devil's party without knowing it." In other words, Milton's Satan leaps off the page while uttering the best lines, becoming such an enticing character that Blake believed Milton may have been used by the devil in order to make the devil more palatable, or even attractive, to the world at large.

Unlike Dante's Satan, there is no pity for this version of the Fallen One. For Milton's version, there's something much more sinister: intrigue, charisma, and, dare I say it, self-identification. Milton's Satan is definitely the antagonist of the story, but there are moments when we can identify with his plight, even though his stated reason for being is the death of all humanity. We too have been frustrated with God, angered by his actions, confused by his ways, and hesitant to believe his truth. At the base of our sinful selves, we too have summoned all of our inner rhetorical skills to fight off the notion that we are inherently sinful beings. We too have waged wars against our brothers and sisters. We too desire the power to rule our lives as we see fit. If we're honest, we too want to replace God.

Milton's Satan accomplished something much more devious than Dante's. He made us want to be like him.

Now, no one would likely attest to rooting for Satan, but Milton's depiction may result in a reader beginning to feel compassion for the highly intelligent, charismatic, confident, abandoned angel. His power play against the Authority of authorities may strike a chord with those who suffer under tyrannical control.

This fallen angel desires power and control, and he's willing to manipulate whomever he can in order to attain those goals. Yet, we're given the benefit of hindsight and thousands of years of interpretation regarding the story of the fall of humanity. Adam and Eve didn't know Satan's ulterior motives. Believing his lies and desiring to know the mind of God, they were easy prey for the deceptive lead devil. We may look back on them with scorn now, wondering how they could have fallen for such an obvious ploy. We may be angry with them for their negligent actions that have led to such a broken world. But, we must recall that they were humans, just as we are. Given the same opportunity with the same slithering tongue speaking deep secrets into our souls at the dawn of time, wouldn't we have succumbed too?

So it seems with Walter White. Surely, we wouldn't make the same mistakes as Jesse, or Skyler, or nearly anyone else who's been in his manipulative grasp, but, as the audience, we've been granted access to a much wider array of information. We know, for the most part, the motivations for Walter's actions. We know that he's the one who knocks. He doesn't have to tell us that. We've seen it. We've been more than first-hand witnesses to the atrocities of Walter White because we've almost lived inside his head for years. Though we're still utterly shocked by his actions, we understand why he took them. In a twisted way, they almost make sense. But, as soon as we start to take seriously the fact that *almost killing a child* for your own personal gain may make sense, we recoil in horror from the idea and from the man who perpetrated the act.

So why do we still care for Walter White? Why do we root for the anti-hero? Or, why do we root for his downfall—swift, full justice that will right every wrong he's wrought?

POP CULTURE VILLAINY

Today, Satan is seldom a specific character in the cultural conscience and more an idea of evil as embodied by the villains we know so well: Darth Vader, Sauron, Voldemort, The Joker, Colonel Kurtz, Jack Torrance, etc. While it would be fascinating to depict each of these characters as seen through the lens of past versions of Satan, that would be an entirely different book. However, let's look at the similarities that these pop culture villains have and what that means about our cultural notions of evil. These cultural icons of evil share three intriguing, defining characteristics: deformity, pride, and an inevitable end.

These antagonists are deformed in some way. Vader's deformity seeps through his singular breathing, evidence of his enormous physical suffering. Then again, Sauron is only an eye. Voldemort and The Joker have visible scars, while Lector, Kurtz, and Torrance all suffer from deep emotional wounds.[84] Though these scars may serve as a visual cue that these are in fact "the bad guys," might they also serve as a point of compassion? For instance, when we see Vader writhing in pain in a volcano, we already know who he's going to become, yet we feel compassion for his suffering in the moment.[85] Did such compassion exist when we first heard the Imperial March or later watched Vader kill a man without even touching him?

These villains also suffer from unbridled hubris, believing themselves gods of their own respective universes. They constantly and arrogantly believe that they are the ones in complete control of their destiny. Unwilling to relinquish power in any form, they follow their ego wherever it may lead, justifying every means in order to reach their preferred ends. If people have to die in order for them to get what they want, so be it. To them, death is nothing more than a practical next step on their daily to-do list. At some point, their hubris allows them to do what's unthinkable to most: to kill, even just for the sake of killing.[86]

Lastly, they always get what's coming to them. Justice is always served in one form or another, whether it means they're ultimately redeemed in some form, like Vader's reconciliation with his son, or they're brought down by the hero. Frodo defeats Sauron. Harry kills Voldemort. Batman captures The Joker. Willard kills Kurtz at Kurtz's own request. All work and no play make Jack a dull boy who eventually freezes to death.[87]

On the whole, our popular depictions of evil are less likely to be redeemed than they are to be destroyed. We collectively salivate at the thought of their comeuppance. Seeing the wrongs they've perpetrated against our likable heroes, we long to see the villain served justice in a most fitting way. While we've been conditioned this way through hours upon hours of TV and movies, I'd posit that there's something at a soul level that causes us to resonate with these repeated notions of good trumping evil and evil paying its dues. Again, this notion echoes one of Gilligan's favorite quotes, "I want to believe there's a heaven. But I can't not believe there's a hell."

Which brings us back to Walter White. Unassuming yet menacing, brilliant yet overlooked, Walter White may be the perfect villain, a contemporary Satan who's pulled us into his RV ride to hell.

First, how does he compare to his contemporary villains? Walter's deformity is his cancer. The diagnosis causes him to drastically alter his appearance. Still, it's this diagnosis that occurs within six minutes of the pilot episode, before we've even met "Heisenberg," that causes us to instantly empathize with Walter White. The foundational cause for his diabolical actions is also the strongest glue that binds our sympathies to Walter's circumstances.

As the show progresses, so too do the boundaries of Walter's ego. The final scene in Season 4, Episode 13's epic episode "Face Off" shines a devastating light into Walter's worsening soul. As the camera pans away from Walter contentedly sitting in his own backyard by his pool, it zooms in on a plant known as the Lily of the Valley. Slowly and sickeningly, we realize what that simple image means: Walter poisoned a child. Though Walter's ego sustains constant and unchecked growth throughout the series, it is in this show-stopping moment we realize his confidence in himself has achieved monomaniacal proportions. Eventually, either Walter's ego will have to break or everyone else will be forced to bow to King Heisenberg.

THE NIGHTMARE OF MY CHOICE

The question on everyone's mind in waiting for the series' last eight episodes is not when Walter will get what's coming to him, but how it's going to happen. "Is there anything a man who has murdered and poisoned children could do to redeem himself? 'That's the $64,000 question,' said Gilligan. 'Redemption is a pretty tricky thing. You'd have to be pretty saintly to say that Walter White could be redeemed at this point. I don't think I'm saintly enough to say that.'"[88]

Despite those condemning words regarding Walter's possible redemption, Gilligan related that the ending would be "victorious."[89] That's an interesting contrast, and maybe one that also tells us much about our violence-infatuated culture. Even though we've been coerced and cajoled into having sympathy for this devil, we're now asked to hope for his justified demise rather than his redemption. For those that have watched the series from the very beginning, who've taken the RV joyride through the Albuquerque desert and back, the series' ending has high expectations. Walter White is evil, and he will receive the full fury of what's been headed his way since Season 1.

Alyssa Rosenberg says it well when she talks about how Walter's able to convince himself that certain actions were inevitable, like killing Mike Ehrmantraut. "While Walt's narrowed his universe to match that set of facts, and to construct circumstances in which those facts override all other considerations, not everyone has decided to join him there. If he's Satan, he's rebelled without being sure of his legions in his war on God."[90] This rebellion minus his minions will be his downfall. In losing Jesse's trust, a relationship that was often tenuous because of Walter's deceptive actions, Walter has lost his last connection to both reality and morality.

Jesse will turn on Walter if he learns about the Lily of the Valley plot to poison Brock. Walter's careful steps to ensure Jesse's continued obedience will ultimately cause Jesse to become Walter's nemesis. The seeds for such a showdown were sown when Jesse and Walter fight in Season 4, Episode 9's "Bug" as a result of Jesse getting too close to Gus without killing him. In fact, Jesse may learn the full and awesome weight of Walter's actions in the final eight episodes and come to the rescue of Walter's family. In my best guess, Jesse will protect Walter's family from Walter, but Jesse will die trying to do so. If this is part of the conclusion to the series, I'll choose to believe that Jesse willingly sacrifices himself as an attempt to redeem his own broken bad past. In other words, Jesse's trajectory on the show is the antithesis of Walter's, a clawing toward redemption despite its ultimate cost, a transformation from a lesser Scarface to a better Mr. Chips.

Jesse knows where Walt is leading him, since Walt directly outlined his path in Season 5, Episode 7's "Say My Name." Chillingly, Walter tells him, "If you believe that there's a hell, I don't know if you're into that, we're already pretty much getting there . . . but I'm not going to lie down until I get there." In this statement, we know that Walter's always been driving that RV since Season 1, that Jesse's always been in the passenger seat as an impotent accomplice, and that they've only and ever been on a highway to hell.

Walter White will not die in the finale. That type of ending is too easy for a show this smart. He will suffer the same way that Dante's Satan suffers: alone. Priest and writer Richard Rene said, "Although the final episode has not been aired, it is safe to say that Walter's current trajectory may well end in a personal hell where he is the single, undisputed ruler, simply because he is the only inhabitant."[91]

All that Walter has said he's worked for—his family, their well-being, his own professional respect—will be stripped from him by season's end. He will not die, but he will be left with nothing but an eternity of regret and all the time in the world to think about what he's done. Walter White will fulfill the prophecy of every cultural adaptation of Satan throughout the ages. He will have created his own "hell of heav'n," as Milton put it, and he will ponder Colonel Kurtz's words for an eternity: "It was written I should be loyal to the nightmare of my choice."

Such freedom to choose gave birth to Satan. Frighteningly, free will is simultaneously the foundation of Satan's actions and the glue that binds us to him. The responsibility of free will is the deformity we share, if you will. We're well aware of our selfish tendencies, our human bent toward pride and egotism. But, we don't know what our end will be. All we know is that our inevitable end depends on our current choices. We can choose to be good or evil, to pull back from temptation and seek redemption, or to stretch our grasp far beyond our reach, a gleaming apple just beyond our fingertips.

"I have made a series of very bad decisions."

FATE VS. FREE WILL

IN SEASON 1, Episode 5's "Gray Matter," we're afforded the privilege of witnessing an intense, superbly acted scene involving Walter's family. In the previous episode, Walter told them he has lung cancer, that it may kill him in a year's time, and that he doesn't want to seek treatment. Consequently, the family stages an intervention, a time for them to vent their frustrations with Walter's decision, with cancer, with death, and with each other. Whenever a person has "the talking pillow," no one else is allowed to speak.[92]

Hank talks about getting a bad hand in poker and makes a bad sports analogy, attempting to tell Walter that luck may still be on his side so long as he fights to the end. Walt Jr. calls his dad out for giving up so easily, drawing a stark contrast between his own daily challenges in living with cerebral palsy and his father's fear of undergoing chemo. Marie thinks Walt should do whatever he wants to do, eliciting a surprised "What!?" from her sister Skyler.

Walter and Skyler's exchange tells us much about Walter's bull-headed decision, as well as the show's take on free will versus fate:

Walter: 'Alright, I've got the talking pillow now. Okay? We all, in this room, we love each other. We want what's best for each other and I know that. I am very thankful for that. But, what I want . . . what I want, what I need, is a choice.'

Skyler: 'What does that . . . mean?'

Walter: 'Sometimes I feel like I never actually make any of my own . . . choices, I mean. My entire life, it just seems I never . . . you know, had a real say about any of it. This last one, cancer . . . all I have left is how I choose to approach this.'

Skyler: 'Then make the right choice, Walt. You're not the only one it affects. What about your son? Don't you wanna see your daughter grow up? I just . . . .'

Walter: 'Of course I do. Skyler, you've read the statistics. These doctors . . . talking about surviving. One year, two years, like it's the only thing that matters. But what good is it, to just survive if I am too sick to work, to enjoy a meal, to make love? For what time I have left, I want to live in my own house. I want to sleep in my own bed. I don't wanna choke down 30 or 40 pills every single day, lose my hair, and lie around too tired to get up . . . and so nauseated that I can't even move my head. And you cleaning up after me? Me, with . . . some dead man, some artificially alive . . . just marking time? No. No. And that's how you would remember me. That's the worst part. So, that is my thought process, Skyler. I'm sorry. I just, I choose not to do it.'

Oh the irony of Walter's words when considered one-by-one in retrospect. As the series progresses, Walter doesn't live in his house as often as he lives in an RV, a megalab, or his own small apartment. He voluntarily shaves his head, even after he's told the cancer's in remission. In quite the turn of phrase that may have been intentional or not, Skyler does eventually clean up after Walt—by laundering his drug money and lying on his behalf so that neither of them get caught.

It's also arguable that Walter *is* a "dead man" and "artificially alive." Justice is coming for him, and the only recompense due his egregious sins has to be death.[93] His number-shaped bacon and eggs birthday plate marks his time on earth, a delicious sign that his one or two years of life expectancy rapidly approaches. Lastly, Walter fears his family will remember him as a cold, lifeless, and sick man. Should he die now and the whole truth of his empire-building be revealed, they will remember him as someone much more diabolical, a person to be rightfully judged for his heinous actions rather than celebrated for his brave fight against cancer.

In short, Walter's supposed choice still leads him to

experience the same consequences, albeit in a different manner. This scene aptly summarizes the series' constant wrestling with the notions of free will versus fate. "It's not just that watching White's transformation is interesting; what's interesting is that this transformation involves the fundamental core of who he supposedly is, and that this (wholly constructed) core is an extension of his own free will."[94]

Breaking Bad, as a highly plot-driven and exquisitely well-scripted show, revels in wrestling with if/then statements. It's yet another tool in the writers' proverbial belts that ratchets the tension of this captivating show.

If Walter's professional ambitions hadn't met their end in a high school chemistry class, then he never would have met Jesse Pinkman. If Walter would have saved Jesse's girlfriend Jane Margolis from a heroin overdose, then 167 people wouldn't have died when Wayfarer 515 and JM 21 collided. If Walter wouldn't have sold his shares in Gray Matter Technologies, his former company that went on to reap billions, then he wouldn't need to cook meth in order to amass inordinate amounts of money to provide for his family after his passing. If Jesse would have carried through with Walter's plan to kill Gus, then Walter wouldn't have been able to kill his two largest enemies with one explosive, bell-ringing Tio. If Walter had not left a damning copy of *Leaves of Grass* out in his bathroom, then he wouldn't have been forced to face the long arm of his brother-in-law, one that's been reaching for him since Season 1.

THE SAFEST ROAD TO HELL

As a scripted TV show, of course all of the events are fated to happen, but within the world of *Breaking Bad*, do the characters feel as if their actions are predetermined, or do they honestly believe they're allowed to choose their own fate? Many characters impose their will on others throughout the show, like the imposing, dominating, caustically funny hit man Mike Ehrmantraut. Yet, even Mike doesn't get to write his own last scene, as beatific and shockingly serene as it is. He's just as surprised as the viewers when Walter pulls Mike's own gun on him, shooting him in the gut while Mike's still in his car. The brutality of that murder is exacerbated as Walter verbally realizes his motivation for killing Mike was moot. Walter wanted the names of inmates that could turn on him, and Mike, living up to his loyal surname, steadfastly held onto those names. As Mike stumbles to a nearby river's shoreline, Walter coldly recalls, "I just . . . I just realized that Lydia has the names. I can get them from her. I'm sorry, Mike. This . . . this whole thing could have been avoided." Yet again, Walter's decisions have resulted in someone within his close circle suffering an unexpected, ignoble end.

On the other hand, hitman Mike has committed dozens, if not hundreds, of dirty deeds. Though he distances himself from Walter, the two actually bear much in common. Mike works illegal jobs in order to provide for his family, namely his granddaughter. One of the reasons we start to gloss over Mike's nefarious activities is that he becomes a mentor, of sorts, to Jesse.[95] Still, in the world of *Breaking Bad*, Mike deserves justice for the sins he's committed. It's fitting that such insensitive justice should be meted out by Walter.

Characters make a particular decision, like Jesse choosing to go back to using meth, but they're unable to see how that one choice inevitably forces them into an inescapable corner later on, a place where only one decision seems right to them. It appears as if their free will decisions result in an absolutely fated outcome. Had Jesse not gone back to using, it could be argued that Jane and hundreds of others wouldn't have died. Like trapped animals, they react in wholly unexpected ways, sometimes surprising even themselves. For a series predicated upon Walter's ego-driven decisions, much of the outcome is a result of fate rather than coincidence. But who's really pulling the strings?[96] Do any of the characters' choices really matter?[97] Are they all pre-destined for an ignominious end?

"The central question on *Breaking Bad* is this: What makes a man 'bad' — his actions, his motives, or his conscious decision to be a bad person? Judging from the trajectory of its first three seasons, *Breaking Bad* creator Vince Gilligan believes the answer is option No. 3."[98]

The clichéd phrase, "The road to hell is paved with good intentions" could be a tagline for *Breaking Bad*. A single bad decision can forever alter a life, as Walter's life proves, and as you've likely seen in the lives of people you know in real life. One ostensibly free-will choice can lead to a series of foregone conclusions. In an "ask me anything" interview on Reddit.com, Bryan Cranston shared the surprising and telling moment he thought Walter actually "broke bad." "My feeling is that Walt broke bad in the very first episode. It was very subtle but he did because that's when he decided to become someone that he's not in order to gain financially. He made the Faustian deal at that point and everything else was a slippery slope."[99] In addition to proving Cranston's erudition by way of his reference to Faust, this glimpse into Walter White's psyche reinforces the notion that one bad choice can start an inescapable avalanche. In *The Screwtape Letters*, C.S. Lewis wrote that "the safest road to hell is the gradual one—the gentle slope, soft underfoot, without sudden turnings, without milestones, without signposts."

Little did Walter know that when he told his family he chose not to seek help with his sickness, an altogether different and more diabolical sickness had already overtaken his soul. Over the next year of his life, we became privy to Walter's gradual descent into a hell wrought by his own hands, an inevitable conclusion to a life built on lies, made meaningful by pride, and motivated by manipulation.

In a discussion with Gus Fring in Season 3, Episode 5's "Mas," Walter appears to arrive at some kind of self-revelation, noting the snowball effect of his ego-driven choices: "I have made a series of very bad decisions and I cannot make another one." The frightening Fring, however, dismisses Walter's confession, noting that what Walter did was for the good of his family, and such decisions therefore aren't bad. Unfortunately, Walter heeds this advice from an amoral, two-faced, drug-dealing monster. His acceptance of Gus' reasoning is yet another "very bad decision," even in the midst of Walter decrying his own errant ways. Blinded by ego, Walter can't *not* make another bad decision. Unless an intimate and tragic event pierces his maniacal facade, he is fated to continue on a pre-determined path.

Walter's feet cannot hold firm to the ground beneath him,

slippery with the blood of hundreds, sliding over all, sloping toward certain hell.

CHOOSING MY RELIGION

The entire plot line of *Breaking Bad* was never written out beforehand. Given how intricately plotted *Breaking Bad* is, this is a surprising fact. It either attests to the writers' collective creativity in storytelling or their need to intellectually flagellate themselves in order to find the most intense and rewarding outcome for us as the audience. "We actively try to paint ourselves into corners at the end of episodes—at the end of seasons, at the end of scenes sometimes—and then we try to extricate ourselves from those corners."[100]

For instance, the writers started Season 2 with a distinct image before a catastrophic event. They worked backwards from the scene of a charred, pink teddy bear's eye floating in Walter's pool. Beginning with that singularly unique visual, they went through multiple rounds of discussion as to how that bear wound up in Walter's pool, even leaning toward an Internet rumor at the time that Walter may have had a meth lab in his home that exploded. Eventually, they devised the ingenious plot line of the mid-air collision over Walter's home.

The mechanism, the engine of story, that results in a plane exploding over Walt's house has to be put into motion by Walt himself: either consciously or subconsciously; either purposefully or by accident. And so, it took a great many months more to figure out how Walt was indeed responsible, even inadvertently, for this plane crash. And that's where the character of Jane came from; that's where the character of her father came from. It was a long uphill battle trying to come up with all these ideas that would reverse engineer back into this initial image that we had in our heads.[101]

It's fascinating that two central characters from Season 2 wouldn't have existed were it not for the writers' need to explain how a burned-out teddy bear found its way into Walter's backyard. It's even more fascinating to consider that the overarching narrative of Season 2 resulted from an initial image and not vice-versa.[102] In tying the catastrophic events of the mid-air collision to Walter's negligible actions as Jane asphyxiated on her own vomit, we see that the secondary characters of *Breaking Bad* suffer the most for Walter's sins. They're merely pawns in his ultimate game of chess. Then again, Walter himself is merely a pawn in the much larger narrative being told by Vince Gilligan and company.

In other words, the writers' choices dictate the fate of Walter White, though Walter rests assured that *his* choices dictate his own fate. So, from Walter's point of view, he has free will, but if we go behind the camera, all of his actions have been pre-scripted. In this decidedly "meta" take on *Breaking Bad*, when we push through the fourth wall, we see evidence of the seeming impossibility of the co-existence of free will and fate.

Might God work in a similar way? Could he be an author that knows our every possible ending and has written one most fitting for our lives, regardless of whether we acknowledge his existence? Could he have one particular image in mind for the end of our days, and every choice written into the book of our lives methodically leads us to that conclusion? Could every person we come into contact with be another actor on the stage of this world whom God has specifically placed in our path to purposefully alter our course? Could our interactions with them likewise help guide them toward their ultimate destination?

Though we believe ourselves to be the rulers of our own fates, might our choices already be known by a God who, I believe, knows us to our core? If God created us and repeatedly states that he loves us, is it not too outlandish to believe that he constantly works in the background of our lives, desiring that our ultimate destination be a place of unsurpassed joy? If the final visual God seeks for our lives is for us to live eternally in his palpable presence, wouldn't he use every moment of our lives in order to see us there in the end?

I ask these questions because I do not, in fact, know how free will and fate can co-exist. I believe we can see a glimpse of it in a show like *Breaking Bad* and other fictional narratives. The characters within the story live unaware of the existence of their author, wholly ignorant that their supposed free-will choices are nothing more than the result of someone else's imagination. They fully believe in their own power to choose the direction of their life despite the fact that their path has already been clearly demarcated. Might we be the same?

To answer, we can echo Walter when he held the talking pillow, "All I have left is how I choose to approach this." We can choose to disavow the existence of a greater intelligence who lovingly plots our path toward wholeness, or we can embrace such a fact and live life in the confidence that the Great Author desires to patiently lead us into full redemption.

It's your choice.

"He was a problem dog."

Discovering a Moral Center

Famous psychiatrist Carl Jung could have been describing the two central characters of *Breaking Bad* when he wrote, "The meeting of two personalities is like the contact of two chemical substances: if there is any reaction, both are transformed."[103] Throughout the series, Walter White and Jesse Pinkman are both transformed by their interactions with each other, one for the worse and one for the better. As Walter devolves from family man to drug lord, Jesse evolves from a careless high school junkie dropout to a conflicted, haunted underling in Walter's empire. He may even evolve into the moral center of the show, the one character who may experience some kind of redemption by series' end. Though Jesse's actions are often just as heinous as Walter's, his reactions to his own choices drastically differ from that of his boss.

Imagine plotting Walter and Jesse's moral choices on a line graph where the *x*-axis equals time and the *y*-axis equals "general morality." Though their respective lines would each have deviations, overall, Walter's line would steadily decrease while Jesse's marches upward. In other words, Walter breaks bad as Jesse strives to break good. In my estimation of this imaginary graph, Walter and Jesse's "general morality" scores intersect in Season 4, Episode 7's "Problem Dog." It's within this remarkable episode that we finally see Jesse come to terms with his inner demons.

The episode begins with a brilliant scene as Jesse plays the aptly titled video game *Rage*.[104] In between gory scenes depicted within the game, Jesse sees images that will haunt him for the rest of his life: his murder of Gale Boetticher. Using a gun controller, Jesse's attempts to flee his troubled mind through the mindless playing of a video game actually allow his demons to break back into his reality.[105] When he's killed within the game, he pauses, ostensibly considering his real-life actions. He turns back to the game, points his gun at the screen and fires upon the word "restart." Either he simply wants to keep playing the game as a way to escape his reality, or this is a subtle way for the show to tell us that Jesse wants a restart in real life. Once we view the rest of the episode, this second interpretation isn't so far-fetched.

In a highly symbolic scene, the next time Jesse's seen in this episode he and Walter talk about Jesse's relationship with Gus. Though their conversation moves the plot forward, Jesse's actions during this scene tell us all we need to know about his moral compass. Jesse, who's often seen wearing loud colors, now dons a white T-shirt. Additionally, he's repainting the interior of his formerly graffitied house, covering his walls in white, a stark outer sign of his desire to also change his interior life.

However, this show revels in the gray areas. Another way to

interpret this scene could be that Jesse's simply trying to cover up his sins. Jesus spoke to such superficialities in Matthew 23:27, "Woe to you, teachers of the law and Pharisees, you hypocrites! You are like whitewashed tombs, which look beautiful on the outside but on the inside are full of the bones of the dead and everything unclean." As Jesse paints, he tells Walter that he'll kill Gus, "first chance I get." Has Jesse really changed then?[106] We can't know which interpretation is correct until the series ends.

As the episode progresses, Jesse fails to kill Gus with a vial of ricin, a move which Gus may have unknowingly prevented by telling Jesse that he "sees something" in him. Such words are manna to Jesse, who's far more accustomed to being a screw-up than someone who's respected. In many ways, Gus replaced Walter as Jesse's stand-in father figure. Gus provides Jesse with more respect, more attention, and more responsibility than does Walter. Gus's motivations are not pure, of course. He wants Walter's higher-value meth without the baggage of Walter's ego, so he desires Jesse to become his crystal blue cook. Even though we're aware of Gus's devious aspirations in regards to his relationship with Jesse, Jesse himself remains mostly clueless about that fact. Once his partnership with Walter has begun to deteriorate, Jesse is naturally inclined to attach himself to another person who sees at least an ounce of worth in his soul. Consequently, it's easy to believe that Jesse never wanted to kill Gus, despite the horrors he's witnessed as a result of Gus's own hands.

Jesse desperately searches for an identity throughout the series, and it's intriguing to see how small words of encouragement or discouragement wreak disproportionate havoc on his self-worth. Walter constantly undercuts Jesse's self-confidence, often relapsing into the role of Jesse's knowledgeable teacher. Even though such instances provide us with a discomforting glance into Walter and Jesse's previous relationship as actual student and teacher, these scenes also serve to augment Walter's sense of superiority over Jesse, even though Jesse's chemical knowledge and "professional" skills come to rival Walter's. As damning evidence of Walter's persistent goading, Jesse verbally explodes this barrage of pent-up rage on Walter in Season 3, Episode 7's "One Minute:"

I am not turning down the money! I am turning down you! You get it? I want nothing to do with you! Ever since I met you, everything I ever cared about is gone! Ruined, turned to s—, dead, ever since I hooked up with the great Heisenberg! I have never been more alone! I have nothing! No one! Alright, it's all gone, get it? No, no, no, why . . . why would you get it? What do you even care, as long as you get what you want, right? You don't give a s— about me! You said I was no good. I'm nothing! Why would you want me, huh? You said my meth is inferior, right? Right? Hey! You said my cook was garbage! Hey, screw you, man! Screw you!

Ever the manipulator, Walter calmly replies, "Your meth is good, Jesse. As good as mine." These dregs of encouragement are just enough for Jesse to eventually become Walter's full-time lab partner. Still, Walter keeps Jesse under his control by belittling him in a myriad of ways, mostly through the constant reminder of who Jesse was and the drug issues that have always plagued him. In contrast, as we'll see in the following section, there are others in Jesse's life who tell him that he is full of worth.

Such a duality of existence sits at the heart of Christianity. We are sinful beings bent on self-destruction, but we are loved far beyond imagination. We are constantly reminded of our misdeeds, which requires just as constant a reminder of our actual, rich worth in God. Some may call us by one name—junkie, dropout, loser—while others seek to dispel the darkness with another name—son, daughter, beloved. We live within this tension every day, fighting the same battle that Jesse fights on the show, whether to believe the bad or make visible the good.

ACCEPTING THE TRUTH

The essential scene of this episode may be Aaron Paul's best performance of the series, and that's saying much considering his considerable acting ability. The immorality of Jesse's actions and the seemingly chaotic, careless nature of the universe finally boil over as he attends a Narcotics Anonymous meeting. His impassioned soliloquy about a "problem dog" he had to put down—but in reality about his murder of Gale Boetticher—is an even more telling sign of Jesse's moral journey than him white-washing the walls of his home. To make Jesse's inner world even more noticeable, he's wearing equal parts white and black, a veritable yin-yang symbol come to life as a penitent junkie murderer.

After the NA counselor extols the benefits of not judging your own actions, he asks Jesse what's going on with him. Jesse admits to going back to the crystal, but relates that he's been sober for four days.

While Jesse's glassy eyes allow us a glimpse into the tortured state of his soul, his words resound with a devastating truth about the universe of *Breaking Bad*: "Couple weeks back I, uh, killed a dog . . . I put him down. I watched him go. I was lookin' at him straight in the eye. He didn't know what was happening. He didn't know why. He was just scared and then he was gone." Another NA member attempts to console him: "He was suffering. It was a kindness."

Jesse breaks the truth to her and himself: "He wasn't sick. He was just like a, I don't know, like a . . . problem dog." The NA counselor asks him how he feels about what he did. Jesse humbly replies "I don't know." The woman who tried to offer words of encouragement just two seconds ago turns on Jesse, spouting her anger at his seeming monstrousness. "Who *cares* how you feel? What kind of a person kills a dog for no reason?" The counselor chides her for cross-talk, then reminds the group that "we're not here to sit in judgment."

Jesse's reply is telling: "Why not? Maybe she's right? You know, maybe I should have put it in the paper, maybe I shoulda done somethin' different. The thing is, if you just do stuff and nothing happens, what's it all mean? What's the point? Alright, this whole thing is about self-acceptance." The counselor interjects. "Kicking the hell out of yourself doesn't give meaning to anything."

Jesse's volume and anger rise. "So I should stop judging . . . and accept . . . so no matter what I do, hooray for me because I'm a great guy? It's all good? No matter how many dogs I kill, what, I just do an inventory, and accept? I mean, you back your truck over your own kid and you, like, accept? What a load of crap!"[107]

Once the moral dam has burst, Jesse can't stop the flood. "You know what? Why I'm here in the first place? Is to sell you meth! You're nothing to me but customers! I made you my b—, you OK with that? Huh? You accept?" The counselor quietly but audibly replies, "No."

Jesse quickly retorts, "About time" and leaves. In the very next scene, he's adamantly scrubbing away at the chemistry equipment in their lab, symbolically still trying to clean himself.

THE GREATEST STORY EVER TOLD

"Problem Dog" caused one commenter to state that "the evolution of Jesse Pinkman could very well be one of the greatest stories ever told through television."[108] While there's definitely some validity to that statement, the de-evolution of Walter White greatly overshadows Jesse's metamorphosis. Walter White will go down in the annals of TV history as one of the most dynamic characters of all-time, fully achieving what Gilligan set out to do with the series in leading a main character from Point A to Point OMG. Yet I believe this is why many people fail to properly appreciate the change that's occurred in Jesse throughout the show.

Walter White is such a manipulative character that he even manipulates us. His ever-expanding ego wants us to see him as the focal point of the series when Jesse may in fact be more worthy of our attention. Though the devastating actions of Walter White are highly entertaining, the transformation of a junkie dropout who'd pretty much given up on life into someone seeking moral grounding is far more fascinating and worthy of respect. It's not wholly Jesse's fault that he lives under the shadow of Heisenberg's pork pie hat.

Walter uses Jesse over and over again to commit heinous crimes he wouldn't commit himself. In many ways, Jesse is the more courageous of the two, even though most of the time he's goaded, guilted, or manipulated into action. Early on, Jesse is a foot soldier who doesn't question commands, knowing that doing so would result in losing the benefits of his position. However, as the series progresses and Jesse becomes more and more aware of Walter's actual nature, he becomes more his own person, willing to throw down the proverbial gauntlet at Walter's feet, using that courage he once had to commit murder and turning it into courage to stand up to Heisenberg. The junkie dropout we saw fall naked out of a second-story window in the pilot episode, the guy who ends every sentence with "yo," has gradually become the voice of reason in a world where reason is used to manipulate everyone. Jesse sees and experiences the full measure of his actions, and he fears the judgment surely coming for him as well.

However, we won't really know whether or not to celebrate Jesse's moral progression until the series ends. Will he turn on Walter in an effort to redeem himself? Will he sacrifice himself in order to save Walter's family from Walter? Will he join forces with Hank to bring down Heisenberg? Will he seek to supplant Walter by series' end, becoming the next great drug kingpin of the ABQ, completely erasing everything his soul has struggled to accept thus far? From moments like the "problem dog" confession to the instance where Jesse's the only one to scream "No!" at Todd's killing of Drew Sharp, the young boy who witnessed their train heist in Season 5, Episode 5's "Dead

Freight," it's much more likely that Jesse will break good by series end. His conscience strives to be free of the shackles of his circumstances.

In Season 5, Episode 7's "Say My Name," Jesse wants out (again), and asks Walt for his share of the money they've made in the deal they've struck with Declan, a new distributor on the scene. Jesse wants his money to get out of the game. Walter, angered by Jesse's desire to leave their money-making outfit, attempts to further guilt Jesse into staying, goading him by the fact that he has nothing else in his life to hold onto.[109] Jesse upends Walter's expectations and tells him to just keep the money. When Jesse realizes that the money is simply not worth the high price he and many others have already paid, we can see how far he's come.

One website commenter echoes my own thoughts on Jesse: "I find myself caring less and less about Walt's fate, and just hoping that the series ends with Jesse finding inner peace and being able to live with himself."[110] Collectively, we hope that this lifetime problem dog isn't put down by a lone bullet fired by his mentor's hand. We can hope, and maybe even pray, that Jesse Pinkman escapes Albuquerque alive and moves to New Zealand a redeemed man, gliding over all the atrocities of his past.[111]

"You're a drug dealer."

The Drug That Stops at Nothing

CONSIDER THE IRONY of Walter's ways. Diagnosed with lung cancer and needing chemotherapy and drugs to survive, Walter turns to selling a different type of drug. He slings one kind of drug that makes the world momentarily better for those already living in their own hells in order to pay for his own drugs that make the world momentarily better for his own hellish, cancer-ridden existence.

When you ask people if they watch *Breaking Bad*, those who haven't seen the show will likely first say, "Isn't that that show where the guy from *Malcolm in the Middle* sells meth?" You nod your head because their statement is true, but you feel the need to round out their woefully lacking description. Sure, *Breaking Bad* is about a chemistry teacher selling meth, but that's similar to saying that *Citizen Kane* is about a sled. The fact that Walter White sells methamphetamines is an essential part of the show, but it is not what the show is about.

Gilligan and company use the plot device of meth production and distribution to make us consider our notions of good and evil and right and wrong. It's the backdrop against which a contemporary morality play can be told using characters we may not necessarily know, but can easily imagine the kinds of choices they'd have to face. Our collective sympathy for Walter clouds our view of the repercussions of his actions. It's as if we've become conditioned to accept his modus operandi, as terrifying as it can be. It's as if we've been drugged ourselves.

As we'll see, meth provides an apt metaphor for many of the show's major themes, but it was originally chosen as the featured drug of *Breaking Bad* more for narrative, rather than metaphorical, purposes. While it's not out of the question to suppose that Gilligan and his writers chose this soul-crushing drug for a litany of reasons, their initial choice of meth as the prime catalyst for the show was essentially a one-off joke that became the starting point for the entire series. The joke happened when Gilligan was talking with Tom Schnauz, a writer he'd previously worked with on *The X-Files*.

We were trying to figure out what we were going to do next, because *The X-Files* had just ended and writing jobs were few and far between. 'Should we be greeters at Walmart? Should we put a meth lab in the back of an RV?' It was in the midst of joking around that this idea struck home: What would an otherwise law-abiding person be doing in a meth lab in the back of an RV? That was the eureka moment for me.

And meth makes perfect sense, story-wise, for *Breaking Bad*. Unlike marijuana or cocaine, it's a completely synthesized drug that needs a chemist and not a farmer to make. I liked the idea of Walt being good at chemistry and having a unique set of skills that would allow him to cook the best meth available. And it's also just a nasty, terrible drug that destroys people and whole communities.[112]

In the National Geographic made-for-TV documentary *World's Most Dangerous Drug* hosted by Lisa Ling, the opening voiceover calls meth "the drug that stops at nothing."[113] A Portland resident says that it's "destroying everything" in her neighborhood. An inmate warns, "You cannot control this drug." Corrections officer Bret King, who's seen the effects of nearly every kind of drug on a person, calls meth "insidious," noting that "there isn't anyone it doesn't touch. It blows away everything else out there." A former addict says, "that stuff gets into you and takes you for a ride you never expected." That addict's father gives words to the heart-breaking reality of meth addiction: "It's astounding how everything goes to hell because of a little white powder."

In the last few decades, that little white powder has become one of the most popular drugs in the U.S., with a reported 12 million people saying they've tried it at least once. How did it become so popular? Meth is cheap, powerful, and easy to find. One hit, or about one-quarter of a gram, could be had for as little as $25. The high a user receives from snorting, swallowing, smoking, or shooting up meth can last anywhere from six to 12 hours. In comparison, a cocaine high could last up to an hour and it would cost more. Lastly, the ingredients needed to create methamphetamines can be bought at a store around the corner. One officer even went so far as to say that "if you can bake cookies, you can cook meth."

The key ingredient in meth is pseudoephedrine, the active ingredient in many common cold medicines. This is one of the reasons why meth is both cheap and easy to produce. Through a series of sometimes dangerous steps, a meth producer aims to extract as much pseudoephedrine from the cold medicine as possible. In the *Breaking Bad* world, Walter and Jesse refrain from using "pseudo" since they'd get caught buying such large quantities to fulfill their orders. With Walter's chemistry prowess, he tells Jesse they're going to "make phenylacetone in a tube furnace, then were gonna use reductive amination to yield methamphetamine," to which Jesse enthusiastically replies, in a line much beloved by fans, "Yeah Mr. White! Yeah science!"

The fearsome twosome of the ABQ cook crystal meth, a form of meth that's more pure, potent, and dangerous to create. Called "Blue Sky," "Big Blue," "Blue Magic," or "that blue stuff," Walter and Jesse create a drug that makes nearly everyone in the show break bad. While blue meth has been distributed in the real world, a result of ground-up chalk being added to the mix, Walter and Jesse's "Blue Sky" ostensibly receives its distinct color from the strict and rigorous chemical processes that Walter demands before his near-perfect product is ready to sell.[114] However, its blue coloration is more a plot device (and better suited for the camera) than actual science. Like the real-life example, the unmistakable blue color is a marketing ploy for Heisenberg's product, a way to distinguish themselves amidst a vast sea of whitish, inferior competitors.

THE INSIDIOUS EFFECTS OF METHAMPHETAMINES

What are the affects of such a drug, especially its "pure" forms? Users receive an instant hit the moment meth enters their body. Euphoria, energy, and confidence flow freely. A former addict recalls, "It feels like you have superhuman powers. It feels like you're a different entity. You're all of a sudden more than you were. You're just . . . better."

However, this high of highs can lead to the lowest of valleys. Meth use results in experiencing the hyperactivity of using cocaine plus the delusions that accompany dropping LSD. It's two bad trips in one, a lonely vacation to a fearful place. Meth addicts can become paranoid and violent, symptoms made all too visceral when the meth-addled Tuco coldly murders one his henchmen in front of the stunned Walter and Jesse.

Two of the tell-tale signs of meth addiction are open sores and very poor teeth. "Meth bugs" attack delusional addicts, causing them to scratch at themselves in vain attempts to pick at the millions of invisible bugs attacking them. "Meth mouth" occurs because the drug impedes the flow of saliva. Users don't drink enough fluids, so bacteria and natural acid accumulates in their mouths, dissolving necessary tooth enamel and killing their gums.

Even as visually shocking as these evident signs of using meth are, the most arresting signal of meth's devastation can be seen when comparing before and after photos. In addition to scabs, scars, missing teeth, and open sores on faces and arms, meth addicts' eyes appear vacant, like looking into the windows of an abandoned hotel. They are weary, beaten souls hollowed out by the ravages of a drug they cannot control. To simply see their eyes before and after even a few years of constant meth use is to witness the living decay of a soul.[115]

Bret King, the corrections officer who noted the sad differences of these pictures, was right to call meth "insidious." The word means "proceeding in a gradual, subtle way, but with harmful effects."[116] Synonyms include corrupting, sly, crafty, and treacherous. Each of these words aptly describes this drug, as well as the antihero of *Breaking Bad*.

So how does meth actually infiltrate the mind? What chemical processes occur in the brain to where a user could become so addicted to the drug that it effectively owns them?

Dopamine is a neurotransmitter that rewards us with pleasurable feelings when we accomplish something. Eating and sex are two of the most common ways to experience the release of dopamine. Part of the chemical process that results in your feelings of happiness stem from the brain releasing a certain amount of dopamine from the part called the nucleus accumbens.

Meth is an impostor. Its molecules closely resemble dopamine molecules. When introduced into a person's system, the brain's nucleus accumbens accepts these molecules, thinking them to be dopamine. As insidious molecules, they slyly slip in. Meth tricks the nucleus accumbens to release an inordinate amount of dopamine into the body. One hit of meth reportedly releases 12 units of dopamine, 3.5 times the amount of dopamine released by doing cocaine, or a staggering six times the amount of dopamine naturally produced by the body.

This is why people get hooked. Such intense pleasure for such a long period of time allows anyone to forget the difficulties of their daily life. This drug's evil nature promises pleasure, but only brings sorrow. It promises the world, but steals souls. The addict's first hit can never be matched, that outflow of dopamine molecules can never be equaled, yet the craving for that feeling rises as the addict's ability to experience pleasure falls. Vainly striving to experience that first high again, users "chase the window," yet the window becomes smaller and smaller over time until the drug no longer provides the type of pleasure the user seeks. By then, the user has become an addict.

Meth actually damages the brain. In fact, addicts fall from the euphoria of an abundance of dopamine to the depression of having too little dopamine in their system. Eventually, with or without the drug, they can no longer experience pleasure, as that part of their brain has been devastated by meth. Unfortunately, meth also affects the part of the brain that controls cravings. It's a vicious, insidious, life-sucking, skin-scarring, soul-destroying cycle. In that TV documentary, host Lisa Ling succinctly described the addict's cycle. "The more he used the drug, the more he needed it."

METH AS METAPHOR

Knowing what we know about Walter White, let's consider how the metaphor of meth actually plays out in the series.[117] First, consider the unsubtle fact that actual crystal meth is white, our tyrant of an anti-hero's last name. However, the similarities go much deeper than that.

As sure as hydrofluoric acid eats through ceramic, meth and Walter White likewise disintegrate everything they touch. To plot Walter's conniving machinations would be to see his mind as the impetus for every despicable deed conducted on the show. From killing Gale to exploding Gus and Salamanca, Walter's ways result in the destruction of those who dare impede his goals. What will this mean for Jesse, Hank, Skyler, Walt Jr. or even baby Holly in the last eight episodes? They have all already suffered for remaining in Walter's proverbial blast radius, but none have yet to pay the greatest price for their association with Heisenberg. By allowing Walter even an inch deep into their lives and minds, they've already allowed him to transgress too far. Like that first hit, Walter promises them the world, but it's a world where the bottom will fall out in due time.

Though Walter prides himself on not using his own product and often criticizes Jesse for going back to using, Walter is addicted to a drug of a different sort, one that is as potent, powerful, and dangerous as the Blue Sky he cooks. As we've already covered, Walter is addicted to power. His pride constantly craves another hit. Again and again, he acts in reprehensible ways so that he can be rewarded with respect, a feeling of professional pleasure he never received in his pre-Heisenberg life. He yearns for the same hit of dopamine just as much as the addicts he sells to do, except he's oblivious to his own addiction.

Walter White is insidious to the core. Likely best captured in the provocative pan of the camera to the Lily of the Valley plant in Season 4's epic finale, "Face Off," we know Walter's treacherous ways. He has become so adept at lying that he's able to constantly lie to himself, especially in the first two seasons when he still naively believes he's conducting all of this ridiculously illegal business for the betterment of his family after his passing. When Walter shaves his head for the second time after learning of his cancer's remission, we know he's gone full Heisenberg. The mild-mannered, beige-sweatered Mr. White has transformed into his own Mr. Hyde, a drug-dealing, monomaniacal sociopath with a cool, intellectual demeanor that allows him to escape unnoticed from an untold amount of possible captures. He eventually slips into the world of the international drug trade as if it were just another logical step in his business plan, forgetting to take into account the incredible costs to himself and his family should he get caught. In too deep, he cannot hope to free himself from his addiction.

Meth eventually reveals itself through horrendous outward signs. In contrast, Walter's sickening soul cannot be seen through such visual cues. Though his worsening condition is seen in the way he relates to his long-suffering wife or the terseness with which he responds to his son, the effects of his decisions aren't visible to the naked eye. Still, like the drug that terrorizes its victims while causing drastic changes to their physical body, so too do Walter's actions cause him to undergo an incredible transformation of the soul. Just as he said in the pilot, it's "growth, decay, then transformation."

Walter has certainly grown in stature as a meth king pin, but at the cost of a decayed soul. As we've noticed, fleeting moments occur throughout the show where the viewer catches a sudden glimpse of Walter's fear and loneliness. Knowing that he's gone too far (again), Walter's eyes widen for a few seconds, a telling reveal that he's seriously reconsidering his ways due to the tragic repercussions of his actions. Again, the moment Walter allows Jane to die is one of the best examples of Bryan Cranston's nuanced portrayal of a man hell-bent on his own demise, yet still barely cognizant of the devastating effects he's having on everyone around him. But, the moment quickly passes as Walter realizes that the cost to himself of not going through with a dastardly deed is too high. The fear subsides as "I am the danger" takes its place. We may not be able to visibly see Walter's transformation from average joe to power-hungry addict, but we know for a fact that without serious intervention, Walter will never be able to return to being the man he once was.

Meth causes its users to care more about their next fix than anything else in the world. It's a drug that revels in selfishness, forcing users to fixate on how they can get what they want out of life, namely, more meth. As a result, as one inmate put it during that TV documentary, "You get real heartless when you do it [meth]." In the moment, meth users don't care who they hurt so long as they can get their next hit when they want it. Walter, for all of his gesturing as just a product manufacturer, suffers from the same heartlessness. In the moment, he will do everything he can in order to get his next hit of pride and respect. He keeps chasing that first high, which may have been the moment he blew up Tuco's hideout with fulminated mercury. Walter's chasing after such a high may be just as motivated by self-preservation as it is by pleasure-seeking, in a twisted way, but it presents an interesting similarity to a drug user seeking their next fix. They want it for the feeling of pleasure it affords them, and they feel that without it they might die.

Lastly, meth is a liar. It promises immense amounts of pleasure for a long period of time, but its affects wane the longer it's used. A user also justifies its use to themselves, feeling that they have to have it or they can't go on living. Walt too is a liar. How often have we seen this? We know this even from the first episode, as he forgoes telling his wife and family about his lung cancer death sentence. To plot Walter's lies over the course of the series would be a case study in pathological lying. His web of deceit has been woven for so long that it's not hard to imagine a single "W.W." thread would mark the beginning of his end.

CURING OUR ADDICTION

What's the hope for a meth user then, and consequently for Walter White? How can they break their addition? First, they must be able to correctly perceive themselves.

An inmate nine-months clean said it well when she spoke of other users and herself: "They feel strongly they can do anything, and they believe their own psychoses. I believed mine for the longest time . . . until I looked at myself." Proper self-perception is terribly difficult to achieve, even for average people who don't engage in highly illegal activities. Our hearts and minds are often so enamored with ourselves, so adept at justifying our own actions, that seldom can we fully know how our actions have affected others, whether positively or negatively. How much more difficult is it for those who've broken bad?

As mental self-preservation, the mind tends to hide from itself that which it can't bear to name as true. More often than not, a surprising and providential moment must intervene in order to cause the user to come face-to-face with themselves. Such a moment can be when the user almost dies, or when their actions while high result in the death of someone else. So too will Walter be confronted with the full impact of his decisions over the last year of his life. Many viewers believe that someone in his family will die by series' end and that person's death will be intimately linked with Walter's nefarious actions. In that moment, he will realize the full and awesome weight of his life's decisions. He will want to come clean, but it may be far too late. His sins will have found him out, begging for justice to be served.

A popular saying in Christendom echoes exactly what an inmate said at the beginning of this chapter: "Sin will take you farther than you want to go, keep you longer than you want to stay and cost you more than you want to pay." At its most basic level, "sin" is any action that goes against God's good desires for a person's life, spanning the gamut from laziness to murder. While the earthly repercussions of sin greatly differ depending on what a person has done, the eternal consequences are still the same—separation from God.

Sin can be as ravaging as cancer, eating away at the interior of a body without remorse. Unless acted upon by an outside force, it will brutally attack a body until nothing is left but a husk. It will grow and metastasize and take over as much as it can as quickly as it can. Sin is also an addictive drug. It will often reward the brain with dopamine and pleasure and cause it to crave more of the same, yet it will fail to keep providing the same reward. It will cause a person to enter an endless cycle of sin and shame, a place where a person feels remorse about their actions, but, not knowing what to do with those negative feelings, cause them to return to the one thing they hope will make the pain go away: sin.

The best way we know to start treating cancer is to visually see its devastation within the body. Without proper visualization of the cancer, doctors cannot know how to effectively treat it. Likewise, curing an addiction requires properly seeing its affects on the user and those around them. It mandates incredibly difficult and brutally honest self-reflection. So too does dealing with sin. A person must exercise utter transparency with themselves and their own shortcomings, admitting their own faults in many, many areas before being able to turn away from those things that would separate them from God. "If we claim to be without sin, we deceive ourselves and the truth is not in us. If we confess our sins, he is faithful and just and will forgive us our sins and purify us from all unrighteousness."[118]

Will Walter ever come clean? Will he confess his sins to Hank, hoping for lenience, or will he suffer the full weight of his actions and be outed on national television as a chemistry teacher turned meth kingpin? Will the cancer that lies dormant in his body awaken, a physical manifestation of the universe's justice? Or will Walter's insatiable need to feed his ego, to get his fix, result in his own death caused by an overdose of pride? More than that, who else will suffer greatly as a result of Walter's addiction?

A Meth Dealer's True Story

To bring the somewhat glamorized lifestyle of drug-dealing in *Breaking Bad* into stark contrast with its real-world repercussions, I've been allowed to reprint the story of a man who could have been the real-life inspiration for Jesse or

Walter. Drawn into a life of drug addiction and then meth distribution, this man eventually found God. Or, as he puts it, God found him. This man shares his story with anyone who will listen, and rightly so. Though shamed by his past, he's proud of his Jesus. To meet him today, you wouldn't think his past to be so dark. He's graciously allowed me to publish his story here as a testament to the true-life evils of meth addiction and the drug trade, as well as a proclamation of the miraculous power of the gospel to change even the most hardened of sinners' lives.

Growing up I didn't have a spiritual leader in my life. My mom was the only one who would drag us to church occasionally, but that was only a few times a year. Not having a spiritual foundation at an early age and into my teens was the forerunner to an upside-down decade of my life. Moving to a new school my seventh grade year made it tough for me to fit in. I couldn't turn to my dad for help with the new transition, so I had to find a new way to get friends.

The drug crowd seemed to be the only ones who accepted me. Having no real education about the peer pressure of drug use and its effect on my body, I tried meth for the first time. It was the biggest rush I'd ever felt. The sensation was beyond my comprehension. I felt more alive than ever before. I was instantly hooked. All my cares, worries, and frustrations disappeared. This was my escape, my release, and my new best friend.

I began to take it more often than recreationally. It became an everyday habit after the first year of use. My attitude and personality changed drastically. I began living the thug life, which led me into stealing and selling the drug to others. Experimenting with other drugs became common. I did every drug that was on the table, but meth was still my drug of choice. It had completely taken over my life. I would stay up for five to seven days straight without sleep.

After high school, I moved from my small town to a big city. This would send me on an even more dangerous journey with a scary lifestyle. With the big city came the rave dance scene, which went hand-in-hand with heavier drug use. Music became a huge passion of mine and I became a well-known DJ, playing at major clubs downtown on most nights. As a result, I encountered more and more people, all of whom I saw as drug-selling clientele. I was selling more meth and other drugs than I could keep up with.

I stopped DJ'ing to start selling full time. I pushed over 20 pounds of meth every month. My living arrangements alternated from five-star hotel to five-star hotel every two days, my pockets filled with thousands of dollars. As a side note, meth really hones in on the sexual drive. My hotel rooms were filled with women and many inappropriate sexual activities. The sense of power I had from selling was unparalleled. How could I stop this fast-paced lifestyle?

I preferred to smoke meth. I've shot up with heroin and meth, but to me, smoking was just my thing. The ounce-a-day habit physically ravaged my body. My teeth deteriorated and fell out one by one. I looked much older than my 20 years. My girlfriend at the time became pregnant. This event changed my outlook on how my life was going to be. How could I raise a child in a drug-fueled environment? I knew I had to leave the lifestyle that I'd worked so hard to build. I wanted to be a better father to him than what I was accustomed to while growing up. I knew leaving the game was the only option.

After my son was born, I felt a tug at my heart. I was unsure how to handle what it was, but I listened to it. With much trouble and many problems, I removed myself from the fast-paced lifestyle I had once been addicted to. At the time, it was the most difficult thing I'd ever faced. Selling drugs was all that I knew and was the only thing I was good at.

In order to care for my son, I moved in with my parents and changed my number so that my former bosses and clients couldn't reach me. Little did I know the lasting effects of my choices. I'd left behind an expensive drug habit where drugs were always available. At that point in my life, I just wanted to have a small amount. I tried everything from drug rehab to counseling. Nothing worked. The addiction was just too great for me to handle.

I tried several times to take my own life.

I would never wish my addiction onto my worst enemy. I would shake into convulsions and punch holes into apartment walls. Waking up to that feeling every day would make you want to kill yourself. The longest I could go without using was two weeks, then I would relapse. I would do anything to get it. I struggled like that for three years to get out of the game. It was three years of hell in my life. Depression, massive amounts of anxiety, and suicidal thoughts were just about my only friends then.

Late at night in early 2005, I felt that tug at my heart again. I was still trying to figure out what it was. I began to think of God and what I remembered of Him when I was younger. I got on my knees that night and said in a loud and angry voice, 'If you are real, then prove it to me! Take this from me!'

The next morning, on my birthday no less, I contacted my mother and said, 'I want to go to church.' We then attended a local church. I felt so out of place. At the end of the sermon, the preacher asked if anyone wanted to come forward to accept Christ. Out of faith, I got up. Tears immediately flowed. I walked up front with the entire congregation clapping me on to continue. I told the preacher, 'I've been a drug addict practically my entire life. What do I need to do?' He said, 'I have the answer. Pray with me.' I accepted Christ that day and felt a sense of relief and comfort.

The next morning changed my life.

Upon waking up that morning, the addiction that had gripped my life for so long and had nearly destroyed me was supernaturally gone. I wept and cried out to Him, thanking Him for loving me enough to defeat the most powerful enemy in my life. His Grace was all I needed to set my son and me onto a new road of life.

I have been sober ever since that day and God's overwhelming love has given me a new heart and relationship with Him.

"What does a man do, Walter?"

GROWTH, DECAY, TRANSFORMATION

IN THE CHRISTIAN tradition, no person can be so evil as to be beyond the infinite grasp of God. Even Walter White can be saved. Even his sins can be expunged. Even his heinous actions can be erased, though their worldly consequences remain.

This is an incredibly difficult teaching.

One of the defining characteristics of *Breaking Bad* is the fact that show creator Vince Gilligan intentionally set out to make a TV series where the protagonist undergoes an intense transformation. With few exceptions, most TV shows feature a main cast of characters who rarely change from one season to the next, much less one episode to the next. *Breaking Bad* shatters that mold by turning a lowly chemistry teacher into one of the most treacherous, conniving, deceitful, murderous, and callous drug dealers the southwest has ever known.

In many ways, *Breaking Bad* asks one of the same questions central to the Christian faith: can a person really change? When someone undergoes an intense conversion experience, as depicted in the former chapter, much of their life changes. Walter's change results in him being dragged into a criminal underworld. In contrast, a recent convert to Christianity often sees their life drastically change for the better, especially if they've previously battled some type of addiction. Friends that knew them before their spiritual rebirth may have difficulty believing they've honestly changed. Skeptical at first, these friends may even attempt to drag the recent convert back into their old habits.

This cat-and-mouse game gets played out in *Breaking Bad* as well as Walter constantly reminds Jesse of his former ways, guilting him into furthering Walter's own cause. Walter's sinful soul can't bear to see his closest friend make any step toward wholeness or goodness. Both of these men are changing, but they're aiming for opposite ends of the moral spectrum. 19th century Christian minister and author George MacDonald could have been talking about Walter and Jesse when he wrote, "There is this difference between the growth of some human beings and that of others: in the one case it is a continuous dying, in the other a continuous resurrection."[119]

The pilot episode clues us in to Gilligan's intentions with the continuously dying Walter White. The words he speaks as he's teaching his chemistry class are telling: "Chemistry is the study of matter, but I prefer to see it as the study of change. Now just think about this. Electrons: they change their energy levels. Molecules: molecules change their bonds. Elements: they combine and change into compounds. Well that's all of life, right? It's the constant, it's the cycle. It's solution, dissolution, just over and over and over. It is growth, then decay, then transformation! It is fascinating, really."

Yet just like the boy and girl students commiserating with each other as Mr. White delivers his impassioned plea on behalf of the art and science of chemistry, we're as oblivious to the full and ominous meaning of his diatribe since we've only known Mr. White for six minutes by this point. Knowing what we know now, this short monologue provides fascinating insight into Walter's psyche. More than just providing the practical basis for his future business endeavors, these words lay Walter's cards face up. Instead of viewing the world as it is, as inert, unchanging matter, Walter opts to see it as a world in flux, something he can change and bend according to the whims of his vastly superior intelligence. As he's romanticizing chemistry, Mr. White uses three differently colored bottles to cause colorful reactions with a lit bunsen burner. With the right tools in hand and knowledge in mind, Walter can effect explosive change.

Yet just as quickly as he grins to himself for his chemistry-as-life soliloquy, we're directly pulled from Mr. White's fascination with his subject and back to the real world that Mr. White lives in, one where his students don't respect him, his wife constantly goads him, and he has to work a second job at a car wash just to make ends meet. This is a defeated man, although we can tell he was once idealistic about his progress through life. If we aren't people like this, we know people who are.

Throughout the series' opener, Gilligan beats us over the head with Walter's sad, average, grin-and-bear-it life. It is this world that Walter wants to change. When he finally receives his cancer diagnosis, a catalytic life moment that represents decay in all its terror, the audience finally relents. We are now firmly on Walter's side, wanting to see his life change for the better. However, this is just the beginning of a cycle. Over time, our relationship with Walter will also grow, decay, then transform until the cycle starts anew. Gilligan and his writing team play our emotions like yo-yos, consistently toying with our self-identification with Walter White.

As the series progresses, we see Walter grow and decay at the same time. His sister-in-law Marie makes readily apparent Walter's motivations for his actions when she says, "Facing death changes a person. It has to, don't you think?" While his morality still seems somewhat intact early on in Season 1, as evidenced by the macabre pros and cons list he makes when deciding on whether or not to kill Krazy-8, every debased action Walter justifies in his mind and consequently commits causes his moral center to decay that much faster.[120] It's as if Walter's morality has a half-life of one season. By the end of Season 2, we know that Walter's morality has effectively left the building, as sure as he quietly, quickly, and deftly left Jesse and Jane's apartment following her overdose. The mild-mannered chemistry teacher who couldn't even control his classroom has now become a monomaniac who knowingly allows Jesse's junkie girlfriend Jane to asphyxiate on her own vomit.

But, just as Walter White veers down a certain path of destruction, Jesse Pinkman, former dropout junkie, becomes the moral center of the show. As the previous chapter attested,

Jesse may be the one person who's actually redeemed by the end.

Yet, fleeting moments of possible restoration for Walter occur throughout the series. These instances can make the hopeful viewer believe that Walter may finally be turning the corner, coming to the full realization of the awesome devastation he's caused for so long. Unfortunately, fans of the show know that Walter's doomed.

So, if you're anything like me, why do we hope for his redemption? In this world where wrongdoers get punished for their actions, though it may take months or years, why might we hope for the worst one of them all to escape such punishment?

Maybe it's because *we're* Walter White.

ALL HAIL THE KING

If you believed in the strict gospel according to *Breaking Bad*, you'd believe the gospel according to our most pessimistic views of America: Greed is good. Relationships exist to serve my needs. Others cause all my problems. If it ultimately serves my purposes, it's morally OK. Might makes right. Manipulation is acceptable when the ends justify the means. Get what you can while you can. There is no ultimate judgment.

But there's a deeper story being told in the *Breaking Bad* universe, one that's been told a thousand times before in a thousand different ways. The plight of Walter White echoes a similar story from the Bible. King David, the man who once killed a giant to defend his people and was described as "a man after God's own heart," was also a man who carefully plotted the murder of one of his top army leaders, Uriah. David committed this crime in the hopes of covering up his affair with Uriah's wife, Bathsheba, an affair that resulted in pregnancy.[121] David's conspiracy works and Uriah dies on the front lines of a battlefield. David marries Bathsheba and all is well, that is, until the prophet Nathan approaches David. Here's the Bible's retelling of their exchange:

When [Nathan] came to [David], he said, 'There were two men in a certain town, one rich and the other poor. The rich man had a very large number of sheep and cattle, but the poor man had nothing except one little ewe lamb he had bought. He raised it, and it grew up with him and his children. It shared his food, drank from his cup and even slept in his arms. It was like a daughter to him. Now a traveler came to the rich man, but the rich man refrained from taking one of his own sheep or cattle to prepare a meal for the traveler who had come to him. Instead, he took the ewe lamb that belonged to the poor man and prepared it for the one who had come to him.'

David burned with anger against the man and said to Nathan, 'As surely as the Lord lives, the man who did this must die! He must pay for that lamb four times over, because he did such a thing and had no pity.'

Then Nathan said to David, 'You are the man!'[122]

As we well know by now, Walter White is the king of self-justification. Confronted with the ramifications of his actions, Walter capably lies to himself about his direct involvement with the catastrophes that seem to constantly befall those near him. Other people have to die so his empire may expand, or that his family may survive, or that he can continue to live. More often than not, his actions are motivated by all three reasons, each vying for importance in Walter's soul. Seldom do we know exactly what he's fighting for. All we know is that Walter White feels wholly justified in his actions despite the inevitable repercussions they will have for him, his empire, and his family. He may be able to rationalize how his particular manipulations may affect the immediate future, but he cannot know the ultimate outcome of his choices. Such knowledge isn't granted to humans, no matter their intellectual superiority.

For Walter White's story to come to a close, he has to be confronted with the brutal reality of his life as it is now. Hank, and likely Jesse too, will be the Nathan to his David, the ones who force Walter to finally look into a mirror for longer than a few seconds. In some form or fashion, Walter's reckoning will occur as he's brought face-to-face with the incredible amount of devastation he's wrought thus far. Sadly, it may require a death in the family, much like King David lost a son as judgment for his affair with Bathsheba.[123]

But, before we sit on a throne of judgment pointing fingers at Walter White as the epitome of evil, we must likewise look into a mirror.

EVERYONE HAS A DARK SIDE

The subtle gospel according to *Breaking Bad* is this: We are all Walter White, broken bad and desperately in need of redemption, but woefully unable to extricate ourselves from the dire circumstances of our lives. Barring some type of outside intervention, we are headed for destruction, and, in the end, an honest assessment of our lives would reveal that the sole reason for our undoing is actually ourselves. Early Christian theologian Augustine of Hippo said it well in his *Confessions*: "For what am I to myself without You, but a guide to my own downfall?"

Coming to terms with our own culpability in the trials and challenges of life is one of the most difficult issues we may face. Tolstoy famously wrote, "Everybody thinks of changing humanity, and nobody thinks of changing himself."[124] To admit "I was wrong" and to face the consequences of one's actions requires an imminently humbled ego, and such an event rarely occurs without a catalytic moment: a death in the family, a broken relationship, a stark reminder of the frailty of life. Being granted the ability to see our own guilt in light of the actions of our lives is both a gift and a curse. We are damned because of our actions, but if we were never made aware of those actions' effects on those around us, we'd never have the opportunity to right our wrongs and claw ourselves toward redemption.

You may actually be an otherwise good person, someone who's never even thought about trying crystal meth, a person who'd never sail their co-conspirator down the river in order to save their own skin, or someone who doesn't ponder devious ways to ensure that your drug kingdom keeps expanding, but you are still Walter White, a gleaming name hiding a dark secret. "What I discovered is that everyone has a dark side. It might be unrealized, untapped, but if the right buttons are pushed anyone can become dangerous."[125]

Part of defining the gospel necessarily means bringing to the forefront that which would rather remain hidden. Consequently, talking about the gospel necessitates discussing challenging, deep, and hard issues before revealing the reasons why hope still exists despite our souls' conditions. As author Madeline L'Engle wrote, "Maybe you have to know the darkness before you can appreciate the light."

Like Walter, we are dying. Every day of our lives is tragically another day we inch closer toward ceasing to exist in this world. As sure as Walter celebrates his birthdays with pancakes every year, we will come to the end of our days in due time. This is a morbid, foreboding thought, but reality doesn't ask us for our emotional or intellectual assent to its ways. While we can get away with casting our disbelief onto fictional characters—"Why would you do that Walter? Don't you love your family?"—we cannot escape ourselves. We cannot outlast our mortality.

Like Walter, we are greedy. Whether it's money, time, respect, or something else entirely, we are seldom settled with having enough. Part of the American Dream, after all, is the accrual of more and more and more. We buy clothes and toys and gadgets to make us feel better, but they quickly go out of style, necessitating another round of buying. We work 60-hour weeks to bring home as much bacon as possible so that we can feed our needy kids with the same consumerism that feeds us. The cycle of more takes drastic measures to stop. Even when we set measurable objectives of what having enough means and reach those intended goals, it still isn't enough. The feeling of security or safety we thought we'd have once we arrived at amassing a certain amount doesn't occur, causing us to question why we ever needed this much in the first place. Just witness Walter and Skyler in their storage shed full of cash. Though Walter says he's out of the game by that point, who among us believes this perpetual liar? Yet we're so prone to believing the lies we tell ourselves in order to justify our actions that both directly and indirectly hurt those around us.

Like Walter, we are bent. Though our egos may not be as epic, it tramples people nonetheless. Our constant thoughts of me, me, me may be hidden to the world for the most part, but we know ourselves too well to admit otherwise. We may live by the subtle credo of "looking out for number one" that plays itself out in highly visible ways. As the center of our own worlds, those in our circles must orbit around us or risk losing our friendship or respect. Our collective bent toward selfishness is the single greatest obstacle we face with regard to our spiritual lives. Without circumstances conspiring against us to remind us of our actual place before an all-powerful God, we would remain proud, haughty, arrogant and impossible to live with.

Like Walter, we are the kings and queens of self-justification. When presented with incontrovertible evidence of our own wrong-doing, we become like children who've been caught disobeying their parents. We will quickly devise a report on the series of events that caused us to act that way despite glaring evidence to the contrary. In our minds, the story makes absolute sense. We may even believe it to be watertight, but such a story is more our minds deceiving us, attempting to protect us from acknowledging our own complicity in failing to meet our own particular moral standards. Rather than admitting guilt, we often only admit to being carried along by situations and circumstances that, naturally, would have led anyone to the same outcome. We justify ourselves because our brittle emotional states can't handle the weight of judgment.

Like Walter, we only know part of the story. Despite Walter's intellectual prowess, he does not know everything. He still only knows a very limited part of his own story. Human as he is, he only has access to what directly affects him and what he can deduce from the actions and words of others. As the audience, we know far more than Walter does and can almost see how this tragic morality play has to play out. Similarly, we only know part of the story of ourselves. Jeremiah 17:9 says that "the heart is deceitful above all things," reiterating the fact that we can't ever truly know ourselves completely. If we can't understand ourselves, how can we expect to fully understand others, or to rightly ascertain their actions as they relate to our lives?

Like Walter, our sins erode our souls like a cancer. Without some kind of divine intervention, we suffer sins' effects, and those in our lives suffer the consequences of our sins too. As we commit one white lie, the next lie comes more easily. As we lust after another person or desire to buy another unnecessary gadget, that inner voice of morality gets a little quieter. Sin metastasizes within. It multiplies upon itself with reckless abandon, uncaring of what it takes so long as it eventually takes all. It is a sickness we're all born with, and a disease we have to fight on a daily basis. Just as no one in the world of *Breaking*

Bad can escape Walter's scheming machinations, so too can we not escape the damning effects of sin in our lives.

But that's only part of the story.

THE GOSPEL ACCORDING TO BREAKING BAD

We have the word "gospel" thanks to the Old English "god-spell," meaning "good news." The Old English term is a word-for-word translation of the Greek word *euangelion*, from where we get our present-day words for *evangelism* and *evangelist*. More likely than not, you've heard these words, though possibly used in a wide range of ways. Depending on a number of variables, the connotations in your mind with the term "gospel" may range from a knowing nod of grateful affirmation to a dismissive grimace of offense. The word has been misused and abused for millennia. If it helps, consider replacing "gospel" with "good news" any time you read it.

So what's the good news of *Breaking Bad*?

Like Walter, we are human so we are loved. Within a Christian worldview, all are loved unconditionally because of our creation in the image of God. Yes, God loves even Walter White. The tangible view of this love appears in Walt Jr.s' plaintive pleas for his father's well-being while being interviewed on the nightly news about the website he created to help raise money for his dad's treatments.[126] One could even argue that Walter's eventual downfall is God's love at work, a just God seeing to it that a violent, greedy, arrogant man is held fully accountable for his misdeeds that have hurt so many. Anyone can be loved by God, regardless of their actions, but it is a love that has to be acknowledged and accepted. In the most famous parable Jesus ever told, the shocking story of the prodigal son reveals that anyone who humbly turns from their waywardness will be welcomed home with the open arms of a sprinting, all-loving Father.[127]

Like Walter, we still have time. Though his time is quickly coming to an end and his redemption is less likely than Saul Goodman winning a case in court, Walter could still choose to repent. However, this repentance would come at a very high cost we know Walter isn't willing to pay. In order to turn away from the life he's created for himself, he'd have to turn himself in to the authorities and admit to being at fault for a number of murders, as well as distributing meth on an epic scale. As Walter's sins stack upon each other, it becomes more and more difficult for Walter to ever confess the full extent of his misdeeds. To do so would be to unravel his carefully constructed life that was initially built on the positive foundation of securing his family's future.

However, we know that his initial justification for his heinous actions no longer carries the weight it once did. After adopting Heisenberg as a full-time persona, Walter White's motivations changed to what they likely had been even before the show started: money, respect, and prestige. Likewise, by staying within the cycle of sin and guilt, we allow ourselves to build a flimsy house of cards that may topple with the slightest outside provocation. As this tower constructed on top of our own ego gets taller and taller, we become more and more unwilling to be the ones to voluntarily topple it, even if its destruction may ultimately be for our own good. We fear losing ourselves in the process, even if the person we lose is a fake persona. The taller such a tower grows, the harder it is for us to seek redemption, knowing what the costs may be to ourselves. Unless the fall of such a tower results in our death, we still have time to seek such redemption.

Like Walter, an impossible sacrifice has been made on our behalf.[128] The sacrificial death of a selfless person has been a narrative trope for ages, from Dickens' *A Tale of Two Cities* to Eastwood's *Gran Torino*. I believe that one of the main characters in *Breaking Bad* will die by series' end, and it will occur as a heroic sacrifice. Either Jesse will be forced to finally and ultimately stand up to Walter (in order to protect Walter's family from himself) and be killed for his selflessness, or Walter will come to his senses and suffer the full brunt of judgment headed his way, offering himself as a sacrifice for his family.[129]

Such a narrative trope exists because of the most well-known story of ultimate sacrifice that's ever circled the globe, that of Jesus. In Christian belief, Jesus willingly offered himself as a sacrifice, the only person capable of fulfilling all the requirements of a holy life. Christians believe that through his sacrifice, all people who believe he is who he said he is and he does what he says he does can now seek peace with God. Instead of our sin-sick souls, God sees his son's selfless sacrifice. In the simplest of terms, because he died, we can live.

For a man who has difficulty believing in the possibility of Heaven's existence but yearns for the reality of hell as a place where the unjust suffer their just rewards, Vince Gilligan certainly sounds like he might understand the key to the universe:

'We sat around this table talking about every possible kind of ending,' Gilligan says. 'Sometimes you start talking really macro. Like, what kind of responsibility do we have to find a moral in all this? Is this a just universe that he lives in, or is it a chaotic universe which is more in keeping with the one we seem to live in? Is there really karma in the world? Or is it just that the mechanisms, the clockwork, of the universe is so huge and subtle in its operation that we don't see karma happening?' We talk about all that stuff, and then, at a certain point, you stop and say, 'Let's just tell a good story.'[130]

As god of the *Breaking Bad* universe, Vince Gilligan refrains from having his characters verbalize explicit moral statements; he simply desires to tell a good story. Why? Because story is all-encompassing. Story covers morality and chaos and karma and the universe. A good story provides the necessary backdrop for Gilligan to conceivably work out his faith in fear and trembling and for millions of grateful viewers to come along for the bumpy desert ride. A good story coerces the audience into his world, a place where we're forced to ask ourselves the same questions that must constantly haunt Heisenberg: Am I really this bad? Why can't I stop? How did I get here? How's this going to end? Who am I? In wrestling with such questions, we necessarily arrive at specific moral conclusions about ourselves. How many other shows are able to goad us into such deep theological territory?

At its heart, the gospel is a good story told over and over in a thousand different ways, a repetitive though wooing answer for the deepest questions of our existence. From the miracle of humanity's creation to our redemption made possible through the sacrifice of the most humble man that ever lived, the good stories of our world will always win the day. They are the stories we can't help but tell because they come from a place deep within. Our good stories are the antidote to our disease, the salve for our wounds, and the hope amidst our fears.

In Walter White we see the judgment that is rightfully due us, and yet we hope that circumstances or God or the universe or *something* will intervene before it all goes to hell. We hope so because we fear we may share in his same fate. Yet, the gospel provides real hope, even in light of the possibility of such a dark ending. The "good news" is ultimately a "good story," even the best story. Through multitudes of stories, the gospel shouts that grace exists, even for the most diabolical of sinners.

More than that, this all-encompassing grace has a name: Jesus. In this God-man justice and love perfectly coexist. As the only arbiter of truth, what Jesus says about you matters more than what anyone else may say—even, and especially, yourself. The story that he's plotted out for you from time immemorial to the future date of your passing can ultimately be a good story, if only you'll allow it to be so.

Fittingly, the first step toward God echoes a line we know so well: "Say my name."[131]

"I'm in the empire business."

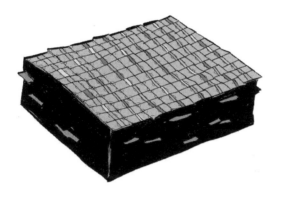

THE END IS NIGH

BREAKING BAD WILL always be in the discussion for best TV show of all time for a number of reasons. For one, the show smartly chose to end the series at the right time, forgoing the opportunity to needlessly extend the series for profit.[132] In a fascinating article for *The American Reader*, David Auerbach pinpoints yet another way that *Breaking Bad* broke the mold for traditional television dramas. Namely, he asserts that the show's focus on changing characters and the fact that it exists within a moral universe required a pre-determined conclusion.

In *Breaking Bad*, the cast has remained small, major characters have died without being replaced, and Walter White's scheming and moral turpitude have reached levels that signal an impending closure to the story. Such a focus on closure runs into two problems:

1. Ignorance: The creators do not know exactly what that final resolution is.
2. Timing: The creators do not know exactly when that final resolution will occur.

Breaking Bad mastermind Vince Gilligan (who also happened to be the second funniest writer on *The X Files*) has enough of a sense of the shape of the series—it's a classic morality tale, after all—that ignorance is not proving too much of a problem. But timing certainly is, and the need to stretch out a clearly limited plot to milk the show's success frequently slowed the last three seasons to a crawl. The beautifully shot but structurally pointless 'Fly' episode is a case in point; any episode that causes a critic to gush over 'the Aristotelian unity of time and place' immediately deserves suspicion. Nonetheless, Gilligan has handled the progression with far more skill than has been shown in the blatantly inept *Dexter*, *Homeland*, and *The Walking Dead*, where the foreshadowed day of reckoning approaches and recedes like a yoyo.[133]

When *Breaking Bad* began airing its last eight episodes on August 11, 2013, approximately three million people started an eight-week journey toward depression over the fact that such an impressive show was ending.[134] However, given the high quality of the writing up to that point, I posited that it would be unlikely that fans would be depressed by the ending. Even though audiences waited an almost undue amount of time in between seasons, and even in between single seasons, I hypothesized that the payoff would have been worth the wait. The stakes for such a critical and popular success were simply too high for Vince Gilligan and his team to release anything other than an epic, fitting conclusion.

"When a show feels like more of a character study, there's more of an expectation that it will end in a correct and satisfying manner."[135] I believed that fans could expect proper resolution, even though Gilligan said that "there are things in these last eight episodes that are going to surprise people. There are also things where people will say, 'I kind of saw that coming.'"[136] It's these "I kind of saw that coming" instances we'll look at now.

As fans of the show, we collectively held our breath for what Vince Gilligan called a "victorious" ending. In the following sections, I've gathered a few theories as to how fans thought the show would conclude, culled from Gilligan's own words, guesses that circulated on the Internet, and my own hypotheses. Now that *Breaking Bad* is over, it's intriguing to see how close—and how impossibly far off—some of these theories were.

Clues to the series' final outcome can perhaps be gleaned from Gilligan's general views about endings. One of his favorites in movies and literature is Francis Ford Coppola's *Apocalypse Now* and the book it was loosely based on, Joseph Conrad's *Heart of Darkness*. The main character Kurtz, at the last, finally realizes how far he's fallen and what he's truly done. 'I'm not saying there is an ending like that in the offing for Walter White,' [Gilligan] said. 'But as

I sit here talking about it, it certainly would make sense on some level.' As Gilligan plays God with White's fate, he'll look to his metaphysical and moral beliefs for guidance. 'I want to believe there is some sort of cosmic balancing of the scales at the end of it all,' he said. 'I'd just like to believe there's some point to it all. I'd like to believe that there is. Everything is just too random and chaotic absent that.'[137]

Given Gilligan's breadcrumbs leading to the series finale, what might we surmise about *Breaking Bad*'s conclusion? From the chapter on hell and the past and present popular depictions of Satan, it was my humble belief that Walter would survive the series, but at the expense of everyone around him. I guessed that he would suffer alone for his misdeeds for a long, long time, whether that meant a lifetime prison sentence or some other fate just as lonesome. If we take Gilligan's words to their inevitable conclusion, Walter White will get what he wants.

So, what does Walter White want most?

At the outset of the show, he wanted to be able to make as much money as possible in as short a time as possible in order to provide for his family should he die of lung cancer. With only a few months to a year left to live, or so he thinks, Walter justifies all of his actions because he's working to provide for his wife, his disabled son, and a newborn daughter. But, as Walter becomes addicted to the power and prestige he continues to gain in the ABQ drug scene, the motivations for his actions take a terrible turn toward the tragic. Forgetting his main reason for cooking, Walter's efforts revolve around the diabolical triumvirate of ego, respect, and superiority. In other words, he does what he does because the ego has an insatiable appetite, never settling for enough, and always wanting more, more, more.

This is awesomely and artfully displayed in full when Skyler takes Walter to a storage room filled with stacks upon stacks of waiting-to-be-laundered cash.[138] Provided with this visual sign that he's made more than enough to take care of his family, Walter then tells Skyler that he's "out of the business" now.[139] Since this occurred in Season 5, Episode 8's "Gliding Over All," the last episode to air before the mid-season break of the last season, we don't know if Walter's being honest about his decision to exit the business that has allowed him to succeed in ways he'd never before considered.

But, we know Walter. We see through his lies as sure as the sun burns his head sans pork pie hat. The pull of the game, the intellectual challenge of outsmarting his drug kingpin rivals, the cat-and-mouse adventure of outmaneuvering the DEA, and the necessity of proving himself to be the smartest man in the room at any given time keep Heisenberg fully in control of Walter White.

What Walter wants most is respect for his abilities and admiration for his intellect. In a projected ending, he would have received both, but they would be displayed for the world to see as he becomes the subject of every TV news channel from here to Germany.[140] In a reversal of a scene from the pilot episode, Walter would be the one on the nightly news as his son asks the same question Walter Sr. once asked of Hank: "How much money do you think that is?"

Astute *Breaking Bad* observer Dustin Rowles posited that Walter actually wanted to get found out, that his uncontainable ego wanted to shout from the rooftops that *he is the danger.*

Whether or not he's gotten out of the meth trade, the biggest question remaining is why was *Leaves of Grass* sitting on his toilet? One argument says it was a silly, accidental mistake, but the other says that it was intentional. That Walt — who is dying — wants to be caught. He wants credit for making millions. He built an empire. He killed a lot of people. He was in it as much for the power as for the money. Would his ego allow him to disappear quietly? Walt is a meticulous man who never makes a mistake. I think he would rather be found out than die anonymously. His ego is too big. I also think the money to Jesse was not just a peace offering, but a message to Jesse to split. Get out of town. Things are about to go pear shaped.[141]

As I stated before, I believed Jesse would be the one to pay the ultimate price. As the bourgeoning moral center of the show, it would have been a fitting, redemptive end for his character should he sacrifice himself in order to protect Walter's family from Walter. Jesse may be the answer to Skyler's indicting statement to her husband: "Someone has to protect this family from the man who protects this family." Jesse's death could have been the catalyst for converting Heisenberg back into Walter White, mild-mannered chemistry teacher—if such a thing were possible in the world of *Breaking Bad*.

In a theory based on Season 5, Episode 8's "Gliding Over All," Dustin Rowles asks an intriguing question based off the fact that Walter could be wearing a wire when seated at the diner counter celebrating his 52nd birthday alone.

Why would Vince Gilligan — who is so obsessed with the tiny details of the show that he once spent hours trying to find a t-shirt with the right shade of grey for Hank to wear — not only allow a microphone wire to be visible, but provide a CLOSE UP of that wire, and do so in THIS particular scene?

Here's my crackpot theory: A few episodes ago, Walter White promised Skyler that before it was all said and done, Skyler would like him again, right? We also know that Walt is currently embroiled in a potential turf war with another meth organization. What would drive Walt to come to his senses, join Hank, and turn on the other meth organization? Two things: The death of Jesse or the death of a child. The signs have pointed to the death of Holly for quite a while.

Holly dies. Walt turns state's evidence, goes against the meth organization (and Lawson, the gun dealer played by Jim Beaver), and maybe he's shot and killed in the Mexican stand-off.

Another potential clue is the waitress' mention of Swampscott, Massachusetts in that diner scene. Why? Swampscott is Native American for 'red rock.' Red has been associated with death all series long, AND 'red rock' is another synonym for meth, maybe the meth that the other organization is selling.[142]

By now, we know that most of this was definitely a stretch, though I thought there might be some truth to it, especially since I didn't believe Walter would die by series' end. Then again, there were just as many signs pointing to that possibility.

We know that [Gilligan's] described the show as a cross between *Goodbye, Mr. Chips* and *Scarface*. We also know that, in the last episode, Walt was watching *Scarface* and ad-libbed the line, 'Everybody dies in this movie.' It would be too easy to draw a connection between that and an ending with a possible shootout in which everybody dies except for the fact that in the season five premiere, Walt buys a machine gun. What was Tony Montana using when he died in a blaze of bullets? A machine gun. Foreshadowing? Maybe. But even if it is, Gilligan would likely subvert the *Scarface* ending, possibly combining it with a faux-*Sopranos* ending: Fade to black before the shootout, à la *Butch Cassidy and the Sundance Kid*. Or fade to black for 20 seconds, dupe everyone into thinking that's the end of the series, then flash forward to moments after the shootout when everyone is lying in a puddle of their own blood.[143]

Brett Martin believed death was the only conclusion as well. "For those obsessed with guessing ahead, it may be worthwhile to remember *Breaking Bad*'s first principles, the nature of the project—charting a man's free fall into the hell of his own worst impulses. And to count the number of endings free falls usually have."[144]

Others believe that Walter's creeping cough signaled his imminent demise as caused by his lung cancer, maybe even as a form of divine retribution for his nefarious actions. Could his actions in the last eight episodes have been more of a race against his own mortality in order to set right his misdeeds? Could he even come close to accomplishing such a monumental task even if he had another 50 years to live? How could he ever redeem himself in the eyes of his family?

In considering what the other characters on the show want, Skyler appears to desire safety for her family above all. Despite the fact she's criminalized herself in going along with Walter's plans, she'll be able to explain her actions as a form of self-defense. She'll be able to say that Walter threatened her to do his bidding or she and her children would pay a price for their betrayal.

As seen throughout the series, Hank pursues justice like a bulldog in heat. Willing to suffer death for the causes he believes in, he nearly becomes paralyzed in the shootout with The Cousins. By the end of "Gliding Over All," Hank finally realizes that his brother-in-law is the man he's been hunting for the past year. Such a revelation boils into conflicting emotions. The justice Hank desired ultimately came at a high cost, both to himself and to those he loved.

The question in every viewer's mind prior to the last half of the last seasons was, "How in the world is Hank Schrader going to take down Heisenberg?" We want to see justice served, but we also want to see these families reconcile because they're family. It's in this tight-knit circle that *Breaking Bad* achieves its most intense character positioning. If Hank weren't related to Walter, Hank's inner turmoil wouldn't be so great and our sense of unease, unknowing, and utter fascination with the final eight episodes wouldn't have been so high. Did Hank want revenge more than reconciliation? Did his professional ambition outweigh his familial ties? Knowing Hank, we'd be safe to assume the former. Then again, his baby niece, his nephew, and his wife's sister must all suffer the brunt of the justice headed Walter's way.

Since Gilligan and his writers intentionally try to write themselves into inescapable corners, the last eight episodes were like Alcatraz. It was satisfying and "victorious" to see the writers extricate themselves from such a precarious plot. How does a DEA agent take down his brother-in-law drug dealer? How does a mad scientist maintain control of his ever-widening empire and ever-enlarging ego?

My favorite theory that could never happen? In exchange for the safety of his family, Walter White becomes a star federal witness, leading the feds to the major meth players. As a result, he must join the witness protection program, where he's given a fake family and the name Hal Wilkerson.[145]

The erstwhile Hal had his own fitting notions of the series' conclusion. "What if he [Walter] created this toxic world around him and, because of his actions, everybody he loved died and he had to stay alive?' But then I'd think, 'He's wrought so much, he has to die. Doesn't he?' But if he dies, what does he die of? Maybe he dies of cancer. After all this other danger! But my true answer of how I wanted it to end, my honest answer, is this: however Vince Gilligan wants it to end."[146]

I believed that however *Breaking Bad* ended, whether in a *Scarface*-like hail of bullets, a final cough on a deathbed of shame, an ignominious local news report of a chemistry teacher gone rogue, the unreported demise of a redeemed junkie, or the unthinkable death of Walter's infant daughter, the conclusion was sure to be just, a fitting end to a morally corrupt man. The writers had to stay true to their intentions, so they had to see to it that Walter's comeuppance bore the full weight of his sins. I'm not so sure the finale capitalized on those intentions, but we'll get to that in the next chapter.

Ultimately, I believed that Walter would assume the throne of his own created hell, frozen in loneliness, a lifetime left to consider his tragic descent. With nothing but time on his hands and handcuffs around his ankles, he'd be shuffling around a federal prison, confused that the cancer never killed him, mad at God for taking his child when he should have been the one taken, and consumed with grief over the trail of death and destruction he left in his wake. He'd awaken every morning and see a ghost of Heisenberg in the mirror, a smirk dancing across his menacing face, tipping his pork pie hat to Walter, acknowledging the fact that it's Walter, not Heisenberg, who ultimately paid the costly price of being in the empire business.

But, in the first edition of this book, I hedged my bets when it came to guessing the conclusion: death, the ultimate arbiter of judgment, may win in the end.

"You want them to actually miss you."

Sympathy for the Devil

When *Breaking Bad* ended and the Internet released a collective sigh of anguish over its completion, this book was updated to consider the plight of the misguided though somehow still beloved Walter White. Who didn't make it to the last episode? Did baby Holly suddenly and tragically become a major part of the plotline?[147] Did Hank's righteous fury rain down on his brother-in-law? Did Jesse break good and turn on his mentor? Did Skyler have to pay a high price for covering up Walter's illicit activities?

Above all, did Walter Jr. get the breakfast he deserved?

Breaking Bad will be greatly missed. Rarely has such a talented cast been convened on a show so intricately well-written and beautifully shot. Through the careful efforts of the hundreds of workers on the show, we were granted access to one of the major cultural narratives of our lifetime, a story about life, death, change, hope, good and evil, family and love and, ultimately, justice and, yes, grace.

Most fans likely mourned the literal and figurative passing of Walter White, but they're not the only ones to have done so.

'Vince, you've had this journey in mind for your protagonist [in *Breaking Bad*], to turn him into this antagonist. As you lived in this world with the writers, did you ever think, I don't want to do this to this guy?'

'In the early going, thinking in Walter White terms was not so bad because he was basically me. On the Venn diagram of Walter White and Vince Gilligan, there was a fair bit of overlap. Frustrations, hopes and dreams, anxieties, free-form fears and middle-age crises. The darker he got, we still shared a lot. Because we all have darkness within us. When he got really, really dark, the more I felt like he was taking me along with him. So many, many months on end—years —of living with this mendacious son of a b— in my head, what's the worst of it? Is it all the killing? The disregard for other people's feelings? The lying? Some combination of all of it? It's been hard, year after year, to live with this guy. There were times about a year ago where I was thinking, It's gonna be a relief when this ends because I can free myself of this guy. But these final eight episodes were different because, not to give away any plot details or anything, but as the writers and I were into a slightly different part of Walt's journey, I started to feel more sympathy for the devil, as it were.'[148]

Like you, I watched the last eight episodes with rapt attention, my still agape jaw extending further to the floor with each new episode. I wanted to see Walter White redeemed, and Gilligan's enticing words above hinted at such a possibility. But can redemption and justice coexist? In a Christian worldview, they always do, and while *Breaking Bad* never espouses any type of particularly religious viewpoint, these characters exist within a wholly moral universe, even if those morals are constantly undercut by ego, ambition, and manipulation. Despite stark contrasts, it is a world still highly evocative of our own. In each world, we want to see the evil ones get what's coming to them and the innocent ones escape with their lives.

There's just one problem with such expectations: has Walter White always been evil, or is he just an innocent man trying to break free from breaking bad?

THIS IS THE END

Perfect. Satisfying. Magnificent. Inevitable. Shakespearean. True.[149]

When the final episode of *Breaking Bad* aired on September 29, 2013, critics and fans alike positively gushed with appreciation for what Vince Gilligan had created. Superlatives flew on social media channels like so many bullets from the back of a stolen Volvo.

"Greatest TV show ever."

"Some of the best television ever produced."

"Every scene was perfect."[150]

Many would-be social media pundits even went so far as to accost Damon Lindelof for his comparatively lackluster and less tidy conclusion to *LOST*. On the night of *Breaking Bad's* finale, Lindelof reported that "my Twitter feed was pretty much a unanimous run of, 'Did you see that, Lindelof? That's how you end a show.'"[151] Haunted by his past—much like a particular character we know so well—Lindelof wrote an apologetic of sorts, effectively saying he's done apologizing to the masses for his perceived mistakes in landing *LOST*'s overweight, overwrought plot.[152]

In other words, *Breaking Bad*'s finale was so well-received that it forced another major showrunner to rethink his stance on defending his own finale. Of the 10.3 million viewers who watched the concluding episode, my guess is that 80% thought something along the lines of, "That *is* how you end a show."[153] Like parents on Christmas eve, Vince Gilligan and his writing team neatly wrapped up a majority of the major plot lines. In a world of TV series that drone on in the endless quest for profit without a particular conclusion in mind, *Breaking Bad* bucked the trend by purposefully choosing an end date.[154] Consequently, the finale, anagrammatically named *Felina*, stands apart from a vast majority of final episodes in this golden age of TV.

One particular word a reviewer used to describe the series' finale tells us much about the series as a whole, as well as our cultural expectations of television, and maybe even our spiritual leanings as a country: hopeful.[155] However, the fact that *Breaking Bad* could be argued to have ended in a hopeful way, to me, appears to negate the world that Vince Gilligan and his writing crew spent seven years creating. A fascinating alternative interpretation of the last episode was put forth by a notable reviewer, a noted author, and multiple viewers, one that better coalesces with what I believe *should* have been Walter White's final day on earth. In a moment, we'll look at why that different interpretation matters in the overall story of *Breaking Bad.*

But first, let's talk about Walter's three sons.

MY THREE SONS

The dynamic between fathers and sons has been fodder for literature since time immemorial. From story after story after story in the Bible to most of Shakespeare's works to much contemporary literature, ongoing battles between fathers and sons resonate with audiences. Such stories are near primordial. For far too many reasons to list here, the father-son relationship as described throughout history provides an alluring touchpoint in any narrative, building a gripping story from the central and integral relationship of a boy and his father.

Enter Walter Jr.

Already beset with the setback of living with cerebral palsy, Walter Jr. must also endure an increasingly absent father. Though Walter Sr. makes every attempt to assuage his own guilt by talking with his son in the few moments he's home (with Walt Jr. eating up his father's attention like so much bacon), the viewers know that Walt Sr. is essentially paying lip service to his fatherly duties. If the camera was able to shoot long enough to show us a literal day in the life of Walter White, how many minutes do you think his interactions with Walt Jr. would actually occupy? As the series progresses, Walt Jr. suffers the fate of a large number of sons throughout the world: an absent father.

And, like a large number of sons with absent fathers, Walt

Jr. pines for his dad. Nowhere is this more evident than in Episode 12 of the last season, "Rabid Dog." Who can forget the searingly touching moment between father and son when the two sit beside the hotel pool late at night, Walt Jr. asking his dad if he's OK, saying "How could I not worry?" The senior Walter confidently replies, "You think I came all this way to let something as silly as lung cancer take me down? Not a chance. I'm not going anywhere." The junior Walter grabs his dad's neck and begins to cry.

Knowing what we know as the audience, I'm not sure if this scene or the one in Episode 14, where Walt Jr. finally learns the awesome truth about his father, is more devastating. Either way, the disconnect between Walter White's repeated mantra of "doing all of this for my family" and the actual time he spends with his family (not to mention the incredible amount of danger he actually puts them in) is readily apparent throughout the show.[156] Why is Walter so often absent? Because he spends an inordinate amount of time with his other "son."

Enter Jesse.

What began as a student/teacher relationship morphed into a mentor/trainee arrangement, then further transformed into a partnership, then ultimately became something much more familial in nature. As Walter White's empire crumbles over the last eight episodes, his one possible tether to redemption is Jesse because Jesse is his last actually meaningful relationship. This is made amply clear in the final scene of the series, but we'll get to that.

Throughout the series, Walter teaches Jesse everything he knows, from the practicalities of meth prep to the intricacies of manipulative lying. As a willing student in Walter's pseudo-

RV-classroom, Jesse strives to perform as well as he can, a young man in need of the acceptance that his job performance may provide for him. A screw-up in every other area of his life, Jesse finally discovers a calling at which he can feel accomplished. Unfortunately, that calling happens to be as the creator and distributor of a highly dangerous drug. Yet this is where Jesse finds his identity, and everything he does (up to the point where he learns of Walt's complicity in Brock's poisoning), he does to please his meth-producing mentor. This may be the main reason why he kills Gale Boetticher, simply to please the father figure of Walter White.

The most tender-hearted, fatherly scene between Walter and Jesse occurs in Season 5, Episode 11's "Confessions," even though the subtly caring nature of Walter White is nearly wholly masked by his ever-present need to manipulate every relationship to his advantage. As Saul, Walter, and Jesse meet in a remote place in the desert, Walter begs Jesse to consider leaving town and obtaining a new identity through one of Saul's many connections. "I really think that would be good for you," Walter says, as the audience hears his words with the same incredulity that we're certain Jesse must be feeling. Sure enough, Jesse finally pulls Walter's mask of pretense away, a moment not unlike any troubled father-son relationship where the son finally stands up to the father.

In a slow, measured cadence, Jesse replies, "Would you just . . . for once . . . stop working me?" With that pent-up reply free from his lips, a tirade begins:

> Drop the whole concerned dad thing and tell me the truth. You're acting like me leaving town is all about me

and turning over a new leaf, but it's really, it's really about you. I mean you need me gone because your brother-in-law is never going to let up. Just say so. Just ask me for a favor. Just tell me you don't give a s— about me and it's either this, it's either this, or you'll kill me the same way you killed Mike. I mean isn't that what this is all about? Us meeting way the hell out here? In case I say no? C'mon. Just tell me you need this.

In a small yet still terrifying moment, Walter stands speechless, then slowly approaches Jesse. The audience fears what may happen. Walter closes in on Jesse, who's openly crying now, and Jesse takes a small, fearful step back. Walter reaches out and hugs Jesse, and Jesse crumples into his arms, unable to support his own weight. Walter holds Jesse up, cradling his head like a father would a newborn. The scene ends, and the audience is left to wonder whether Walter truly cares for Jesse or if this was yet another deliberate move on Walter's part to manipulate relationships for his own gain. As the following scenes of that episode attest, it would seem that it is more manipulation working its Heisenbergian magic as Jesse begins the process of changing his identity and moving to Alaska.[157] Yet, as we know by series' end, a small part of Walter's shattered soul still beats with the heart of a father looking out for his son.

But Walter has still one more "son," a veritable heir to the throne of his empire.

Enter Todd.

Despite being warned to only speak when spoken to, Todd Alquist sets himself apart from his Vamonos Pest Control brethren by telling Walter he disabled a nanny cam in the first "fumigated" home Walter and Jesse cook in. From that early introduction, the audience is keyed into the fact that Todd may have more work to do as the series progresses.

As Walter continues to bring Todd closer into his work, an intriguing dynamic between Todd and Jesse forms. When Todd coldly shoots Drew Sharp, the young boy on a motorcycle who happened upon the great train heist—despite the plaintive, wailing cry from Jesse to stop—the audience comes to the devastating awareness that Todd isn't simply another minion in Walter's empire. He's a callous murderer who wants nothing more than to prove his worth to Walter.

Todd finally ascends to Walter's inner circle after Mike and Jesse opt to quit working with Walter, fearful that Walter's pride would lead them all to certain death, or at least a long, long jail sentence. In an echo of seasons' past, Walter teaches Todd everything he knows about making meth. It's through Todd that Walter becomes connected with Todd's Uncle Jack, a Neo-Nazi leader with connections to nefarious people who ultimately killed 10 of Mike's guys in prison who knew about Walter's ways. When Walter finally opts out of the game, Todd still cooks. He assumes the throne of the empire.

Todd embodies the logical legacy of Heisenberg; he's everything that Walter White's superego wishes it could be. Though Todd's granted a bit of humanity in his infatuation with Lydia, he's able to separate his emotions from the task at hand, as evidenced by his cruel murdering streak, his deadpan way of speaking, and the devastating way he tortures Jesse. Especially in the last few episodes, it's made readily apparent that Todd is Jesse's foil, the antithesis to Jesse's emotionally charged moral center. Todd has no moral center, and he never allows emotion to overcome him.

These stories of warring sons are reminiscent of many found throughout history, but especially within the Bible. At the beginning of time, Cain kills his brother Abel, jealous over his acceptance by God. Later, Jacob steals Esau's birthright, imitating his hairy brother by wearing goatskin. Joseph's brothers literally sell him down the river, refusing to kill him, but rather offering him as a slave to a wandering Midianite nomad headed for Egypt. The enmity that can exist between brothers can be as strong as, if not stronger than, the close bond that amiable brothers might enjoy. And, many of these stories can be traced back to one innate, much sought after need: to feel a father's pride.

Walt Jr., Jesse, and Todd, though buffeted by a multitude of extraneous motivations, all share the same need to prove their worth to a father figure. Early on in the series, Walt Jr. creates a website to help offset his father's medical expenses. Jesse works as hard as he can to follow the lead of his teacher and mentor as he learns the business. Todd desires so desperately to be useful that he seldom thinks before he acts, an automaton of mayhem. Somewhat surprisingly, Walt Jr. never meets Jesse or Todd, which one has to assume would have been both an awkward yet tense moment had they ever convened. Knowing what he knows by series' end, is it possible that Walt Jr. would have attacked Jesse in the same way that Jesse attacked Todd? Is it possible that he would have transferred all of his hatred for his father to Jesse, the "son" that Walter Sr. effectively adopted as his own considering how much time they spent together?

Walter's interactions with his three "sons" provide yet

another window into his tortured soul. Loved and appreciated yet manipulated and lied to, all three of them eventually suffer a cataclysmic loss for their involvement with a dad too selfish to recognize the immense errors of his ways. Echoing Cain and Abel, Todd dies from Jesse's justifiably vengeful hands. Walt Jr. loses the father he never really had in the first place, at least for the last few years of his life. Over the last episodes of the final season, Jesse loses nearly everything, culminating in the cold-blooded murder of Andrea that he's forced to watch. Though his father figure ultimately sacrificed himself to set Jesse free, cutting the literal chain that had been tying down that rabid dog, one has to wonder if Jesse considered even that sacrifice enough recompense to make up for the hell that Walter White made him endure.

THE END THAT SHOULD HAVE BEEN

When asked by GQ Magazine how he thought *Breaking Bad* should end, Bryan Cranston said, "However Vince Gilligan wants it to end."[158]

In an interview about Season 5, Episode 16's finale, "Felina," Vince Gilligan said, "I think plenty of people out there will have had a different ending for this show in their mind's eye and therefore we're bound to disappoint a certain number of folks, but I really think I can say with confidence that we made ourselves happy and that was not remotely a sure thing for the better part of a year. I feel that the ending satisfies me and that's something that I'm happy about."[159]

To be honest, I count myself as a member of "a certain number of folks." The finale of *Breaking Bad* didn't sit well with me, and in the moments following its epic ending, I didn't understand the small twinge of a slight letdown I felt. Though "Felina" was fascinating, well-acted, smartly paced, and very effective in wrapping up existing plot lines, one major issue bothered me. I couldn't identify the exact reason until I read Emily Nussbaum's article "The Closure-Happy 'Breaking Bad' Finale." After applauding the finale for making a majority of its fans happy, Nussbaum posits a different ending, one wholly in line with what I thought should have happened (emphasis added):

> I did not like the episode. Maybe it was just me . . . but halfway through, at around the time that Walt was gazing at Walt, Jr., I became fixated on the idea that what we were watching must be a dying fantasy on the part of Walter White, not something that was actually happening —at least not in the 'real world' of the previous seasons.
>
> And, if that were indeed the case, I'd be writing a rave.
>
> **I mean, wouldn't this finale have made far more sense had the episode ended on a shot of Walter White dead, frozen to death, behind the wheel of a car he couldn't start?**[160]

Noted author Joyce Carol Oates agreed: "Did anyone think that Walter White is 'posthumous' through the final episode? Appears like a ghost through locked doors? Fantasy revenge?"[161] Comedian Norm MacDonald sent out multiple tweets a few days after the series finale, pointing out a number of instances within "Felina" that undergird his hypothesis of a hypothermic Heisenberg. In one, he agrees with Oates' notice of Heisenberg's ghost-like qualities in the finale. "He's the most wanted man there is, but he eats at a diner and chats with a waitress and appears wherever he wants."[162] If you'll recall, Marty Robbins' song "El Paso" played an integral role in the series finale, the least of which was providing lyrical inspiration for the title of the final episode. MacDonald points to that song as yet another reason why Walter must have been dead throughout a majority of "Felina." "The important thing to remember about the song El Paso was that the guy singing it was DEAD."[163]

MacDonald ultimately stakes his claim to his interpretation of the ending. "One thing seems clear. He never made it out of that car in the snow, surrounded by police. That's where he died, his final prayer unanswered."[164] Despite these well-intentioned and seemingly plausible alternate interpretations of the ending, Vince Gilligan has flatly stated that the finale was not a dream, "because Walt would therefore have to be dreaming about things he would otherwise have no knowledge of."[165] From a viewer's perspective, the dream sequence finale interpretation also flies in the face of *Breaking Bad*'s overall narrative, a story told "as is" that inhabits reality in a way that few other television shows ever have, so much so that fans in Albuquerque gave Walter White a real-life funeral.[166]

The central question behind the conspiracy theory of a dying Walter's revenge fantasy is whether or not he deserved to be able to set right what little he could set right. It's a question of atonement, as well as a question of whether or not justice was ultimately served in his death. In my opinion, the conclusion as portrayed on screen ultimately redeems Walter, and that seems a direct contradiction to the infamously well-known intentions of the show, "to turn Mr. Chips into Scarface." Tony Montana dies an ignominious death, unable to save his sister or completely obliterate his enemies. In contrast, Walter White makes amends with his estranged wife, says goodbye to the daughter he once kidnapped, provides millions in drug money to a son that despises him, annihilates every last one of his enemies, *and* effectively sacrifices himself to save the one associate he manipulated the most throughout the entire series.

In other words, it's Walter White in the finale, not Heisenberg.[167] The finale provides ample visual evidence of this, what with Walter wearing a beige coat and khakis that echo his high school teaching days and forgoing his iconic pork pie hat. The audience is even more keyed into this fact when Walter finally offers a true confession, one that cuts directly against his fabricated confession condemning Hank in Season 5, Episode 11's "Confessions." In the finale, Walter stuns Skyler (and the audience) when he finally admits what we've all known since Episode 1: "Everything I did, I did it for . . . me. I liked it. I was good at it. And I was . . . alive."[168]

The possibility for an alternative interpretation of the finale as outlined above stems from a unique moment that occurs early on in "Felina." As Walter climbs into an iced over car and fails to hot-wire it, he prays. Never before in the series has he spoken words of supplication in any way. He's never uttered words that would appear to ask for help from a nameless source. Throughout the entirety of *Breaking Bad*, Walter White has relied solely on himself. His superior intellect has always been the answer to his own prayers. But, in "Felina," Walter humbly pleads to no one in particular, "Just get me home. I'll do the rest." So desirous is he to make amends for the crimes he's committed that he asks for help from God or a Higher Power or the universe itself. Surprisingly, the answer to his prayer literally falls out of the sky as the keys to the car roll down from the visor like manna from heaven. This is the catalytic moment that allows Walter to accomplish everything his dying heart desires.

However, like many whose prayers are answered in short order (this author included), a smirk crosses Walter's face as soon as the keys drop into his lap, a telling facial tic that could imply Walter thinking something along the lines of "The world still bends to me." In other words, his prayer *had* to be answered because he's about to embark on a just cause. Maybe the universe swings itself to help Walter's cause because, as Vince Gilligan stated so long ago, "karma kicks in at some point."

Yet this is one of the reasons, if not the main reason, that the all-too-tidy conclusion seems too neat, even for the oftentimes fastidious Walter White.

THE REDEMPTION OF WALTER WHITE

If you've been reading this book closely, you might have noticed a glaring discrepancy.

I began *The Gospel According to Breaking Bad* hoping for Walter's redemption. I ended *The Gospel According to Breaking Bad* championing an alternative interpretation of the conclusion that goes against the "redemptive" finale. The hard question I'm left to answer is, did I truly want to see Walter redeemed? The question behind that question is, where does the line between justice and grace exist?

Let's look at Vince Gilligan's words again in the quote that became the catalyst for this book: "I feel some sort of need for biblical atonement, or justice, or something. I like to believe there is some comeuppance, that karma kicks in at some point, even if it takes years or decades to happen." Walter does indeed pay the highest price for his sins—death—but instead of karma leaving Walter frozen in a Volvo, grace allows him to essentially make amends with those he's hurt the most. This echoes Bono's line, "Along comes this idea called Grace to upend all that 'as you reap, so you will sow' stuff. Grace defies reason and logic. Love interrupts, if you like, the consequences of your actions."

So why is Walter even allowed to escape the cold and lonely confines of his New Hampshire cabin prison in order to set his world as right as he can? He finally acknowledged his selfish intentions. As I stated earlier, "For redemption to even be a possibility, the sin must be acknowledged by the one at fault and recognized for its evil grasp on the sinner and its devastation on those around them." In confessing his "aliveness" to Skyler while donning Heisenberg's unmistakable pork pie hat, Walter finally realized what Jesse showed him many episodes ago: "You either run from things, or face them, Mr. White. It's all about accepting who you really are. I accept who I am." Walter then asks Jesse, "And who are you?" Jesse replies, "I'm the bad guy." Walter had to run all the way across the country before coming to terms with the cataclysmic devastation of his actions before finally being able to see himself as "the bad guy." Walter's realization of his own depravity allows room within his soul for grace to invade.

When I wrote the following lines prior to the last eight episodes, I didn't realize how prescient they would be: "By the end of *Breaking Bad*, the notion of love will play an intricate and important role in its conclusion, either as a saving grace for Walter or his family, or a final motivation for justice to extract its ultimate payment from Walter." Love plays an immensely important role in the finale, but not remotely in the way I expected. Such love is seen in two diametrically opposed ways.

As evidenced by the final scene of the series, as Walter lovingly places his hand on a vat in the cook room where Jesse was forced to work, we realize what Walter idolized the most during the last few years of his life: the craft. His newfound work brought meaning and purpose to his otherwise beige life. The conclusion further reinforces this notion as Badfinger's "Baby Blue" blares over Walter's death scene with startling chords and fitting words: "Guess I got what I deserved / Kept you waiting there too long, my love / All that time without a word / Didn't know you'd think that I'd forget or I'd regret / The special love I had for you, my baby blue."[169] Walter's adoration of his life's highest achievement is also stated in the final lines of Marty Robbins' song "El Paso," which played at the beginning of the episode, as well as during Walter's *MacGuyver*-like scene as he creates the pop-up garage door machine gun. "From out of nowhere Felina has found me / Kissing my cheek as she kneels by my side / Cradled by two loving arms that I'll die for / One little kiss and Felina, goodbye." If we're still unsure of Walter's true affections, Gilligan's descriptions in the script for "Felina" leave little doubt as to Walter's idol:

In post-*Breaking Bad* interviews, Gilligan has often labeled Walter White's cooking equipment with a *Lord of the Rings* reference, calling the lab 'his precious.' And that statement is echoed in the script during the closing scene of Walt gently stroking the equipment in the Nazis' lab: 'Walt is back where belongs,' he writes. 'He's back with his True Love.' Gilligan pens Walt's death scene as a tender embrace between two old friends, describing his final facial expression as 'one of faint satisfaction.'[170]

So, without a doubt, we know what Walter loved more than anything else: the craft that became so integral to his existence that it came to define him despite devastating his world. In other words, he loved himself and what his superior mind was able to accomplish. Still, I thought that Walter's love for his family might have trumped his ultimate end game, that somehow his repeated statements of "doing all of this for my family" would eventually come true. Though that love motivated much of his action in the finale as he sought to make amends with his wife and children, it was not the central love portrayed in the finale.

I never thought that Walter's love for Jesse was real and would ultimately cause him to sacrifice himself for Jesse's freedom. I assumed Walter's hubris was too grandiose for such an act. This self-sacrificial moment works to redeem Walter in a way, especially after how much Jesse suffered at the hands of Odd Todd and his Uncle Jack. By series' end, thankfully, Jesse is the only one to have experienced true, literal redemption, as he's freed from the shackles that had enslaved him for so long. While we'll never know exactly how Jesse will come to terms with the last few years of his life under the terrifying tutelage of Mr. White, Gilligan's script for the finale relates that Jesse's future is hopeful: "From here on, it's up to us to say where he's headed . . . I like to call it 'something better' and leave it at that."[171] *Breaking Bad* fans the world over either cried in delight or exhaled a long pent up sigh of relief as Jesse screamed out of the compound toward an unknown, but free, future.

Despite Jesse's epic escape, where the rabid problem dog finally broke loose for good, his story was ultimately overshadowed by the monumental tale of Walter White. Even though Jesse's redemption by Walter's sacrifice ultimately proved Walter's true affections for his former pupil, I don't think that was the central theme of love portrayed in the show either. It was, however, a consequence of the grand love shown to Walter White in the series finale by an unexpected source: Vince Gilligan.

Earlier I stated that "God loves even Walter White." It's a statement that's easy to write, yet still challenging for me to fully understand. How could a perfect God love a supremely imperfect soul like Walter White? How could someone so diabolical still have a hope of heaven despite their hellish life? Surprisingly and shockingly, *Breaking Bad* offers us a glimpse into such challenging theology.

Vince Gilligan loves Walter White. Though he may vehemently disagree with Walter's actions, he ultimately wants to see Walter redeemed because Walter is his creation. To Vince, Walter is the Jesse to his Walter. In other words, Vince wants to set Walter free from the shackles of his life in the same way that Walter freed Jesse. Since Vince Gilligan is the god of the *Breaking Bad* universe, he alone holds the power to grant grace to Walter White. By answering Walter's prayer in the final episode, Gilligan allows his most cherished creation to seek redemption.

Through *Breaking Bad*'s five seasons, I discovered that I'm fascinated by the things of this world that can consume us to the point of changing our identity. Though our actions wildly differed, I could still see myself in the mirror that Walter's devious ways placed before me every Sunday night. As much as I wanted to resist such an awful comparison, I was forced to realize that my own shortcomings in life found their genesis in the same issues that plagued Walter White to his core, like his greed, selfishness, and pride, to name a few.

As the series progressed and Walter continued to doggedly pursue his selfish ambitions, even to the point of both literally and figuratively losing family members, my sympathies for that devil waned to the point that I desired him to suffer greatly for the sins he'd committed. I thought that death would have been too simple of an escape, a judgment that couldn't have equaled the justice due his egregious sins. Consequently, when the series ended with Walter's death, I felt anger at the fact that he was, arguably, going to "get away" with it.[172] Later, I felt shame at my own condemnation of Walter. If I truly believe that anyone can be saved, why did I want to see Vince Gilligan and his writers serve Walter his just rewards without remorse?

I eventually realized that my reactions epitomized an intensely selfish desire: I want to see justice served when others transgress, but I want grace to invade my own life. Like Vince Gilligan, I want to see the wrongs of the world righted in some way, the Idi Amins and Saddam Husseins and Osama bin Ladens brought to swift and terrible justice, Old Testament style. By the way that Vince had spoken about the show for so long, in transforming Walter into Scarface, I assumed the finale would be as devastating in its meting out of judgment as the show had been in its portrayal of violence. When Vince Gilligan effectively flipped the script on my expectations of the ending, he upset my idea of how I thought his world should work.

But this is the way I think the real world *does* work. Justice and grace coexist. They sidle next to each other in ways we can seldom fathom, in ways that may cause us to question a death-row inmate's last-minute confession, in ways that may ire morally superior (but still corrupted) humans who fail to extend grace to those who need it most. Gilligan metes out both justice and grace in the finale. Walter paid the ultimate price for his wrongdoings, but was granted the time to perform a number of last acts of contrition, a series of moves that arguably worked as expiation for his sins, the most satisfying of which was his self-sacrifice to free Jesse.[173]

As I stated before, the gospel shouts that grace exists. If such grace can break into the dark confines of a show like *Breaking Bad*, it can surely invade your life as well. The justice due you may still find its way to your door, but the caring, careful love of the God who made you may still rain grace upon you, dropping it into your lap like a set of Volvo keys at the exact moment you need them.

ABOUT THE AUTHOR

BLAKE ATWOOD IS an editor, writer, and unabashed fan of Jesus, *Breaking Bad,* and the Oxford comma.

Connect with him online at
BlakeAtwood.com.

Continue the conversation about *The Gospel According to Breaking Bad*, or visit the websites linked to in the footnotes, at
blakeatwood.com/breaking-bad

To report any factual errors or typos, or to discuss the show or this book, email **breakingbad@blakeatwood.com**

Twitter: twitter.com/batwood
Facebook: facebook.com/blake.atwood.writer
Google+: plus.google.com/+blakeatwood

THANK YOU

... TO MY EVER-patient, ever-beautiful, ever-joyful, ever-encouraging, ever-loving, ever-loved wife.

... to my quickly-working and quite adept editor, Alise Wright.

... to Wes Molebash for providing stellar illustrations.

... to my supportive co-workers at FaithVillage.

... to my family and friends, for *always* telling me I should write a book someday.

... to Mrs. Sloman's fourth grade classes for ~~guilting me into~~ encouraging me to write a book.

... to Vince Gilligan, his crew, and his cast, for creating a fascinating world that millions of us were sad to see ride off into the Albuquerque desert.

... to *you*, for taking the time to buy and read this book. May it help you further enjoy ~~one of~~ the best TV series of all time.

[1] "It was one of those rare moments when you respond to a piece of material so strongly that I knew I had to get in as fast as I could to try to get this role, because the longer I waited, I knew that every actor in Hollywood would want to be a part of this, and fortunately I was the one to get it." — Bryan Cranston, video excerpt, The Paley Center for Media, "Bryan Cranston on the Shocking Pilot Script."

[2] Alan Sepinwall, *The Revolution Was Televised: The Cops, Crooks, Slingers and Slayers Who Changed TV Drama Forever.*

[3] *Breaking Bad* was also nominated for the same award in its first two seasons, but lost to *Mad Men*. One has to wonder if Walter White would ever slip ricin into one of Don Draper's many, many drinks for this affront to his ego.

[4] Though the style of *Mad Men* and *Breaking Bad* greatly differ, it's interesting to note much of their substance is the same: pride, manipulation, dual lives, questionable morality, etc. However, that's fodder for someone else's book to consider.

[5] David Segal, "The Dark Art of *Breaking Bad*"

[6] Chuck Klosterman, "*Bad* Decisions" / We all know that Chuck's smart, but when he says that *Breaking Bad* is the best series of all time, I'm prone to vault him to "brilliant" status.

[7] I hope you will, and if you're reading this footnote, I'm guessing you're going to, so thanks!

[8] A Christian inside joke of sorts. Sunday night services, at least where I came from, were sparsely attended, allowing the naive believers who did attend (like me) to think that they were better than everyone else. Yes, it took me a long time to think otherwise.

[9] Oh the follies of youth.

[10] I was *the life* of every party I never attended.

[11] The reason the Simpsons are yellow? Show creator Matt Groening wanted viewers to think the color settings on their TV sets were askew.

[12] Wholesale slaughters of innocents. Crucifixions. Stonings. It's a long list. For insight into the troublesome issue of violence in the Bible, read David T. Lamb's *God Behaving Badly*.

[13] Please don't misconstrue this section as having anything to do with race. I realize that many people have drastically different words spring to mind with regard to the word "white."

[14] Mike Flaherty, "The Showrunner Transcript: *Breaking Bad*'s Vince Gilligan on Season Four and His Experiences on *The X-Files*"

[15] Nicole LaPorte, "The 100 Most Creative People in Business 2013: 8: Bryan Cranston," pg. 80, *Fast Company, June 2013*

[16] Though the footage never made it onto the show, Bryan Cranston actually shaved his head in Season 1, Episode 6, where Walter White shaves his head for the first time. In an act of solidarity, Vince Gilligan also shaved his head, as did many other crew members. According to Gilligan, Cranston shaved many of the crew and became quite adept at the task. AMCtv.com video, "Walt Goes Bald: Inside *Breaking Bad*"

[17] "I Am Bryan Cranston, AMA"

[18] Brett Martin, "The Last Stand of Walter White"

[19] American Institute of Physics, "Quantum Mechanics: The Uncertainty Principle"

[20] "Naked I came from my mother's womb, and naked I will depart. The Lord gave and the Lord has taken away; may the name of the Lord be praised." - Job 1:21

[21] The Internet Surname Database, "Schrader"

[22] Behind the Name, "Hank"

[23] Still, I didn't think *Breaking Bad* would end with Walter's death. More on that later.

[24] R. Alan Orange, "AMC Plans *Breaking Bad* Saul Goodman Spin-Off." The fact that the writers talked about a spin-off tipped their hand to at least one fact about the last eight episodes of *Breaking Bad*: Goodman survives.

[25] Your eyes will hate you for it, but your fandom requires at least one visit to www.bettercallsaul.com.

[26] Lane Brown, "In Conversation: Vince Gilligan on the End of *Breaking Bad*"

[27] If you'll recall, this "fugue state" was yet another lie cooked up by Walter in order to disguise his kidnapping by Tuco and his subsequent escape back to suburbia.

[28] AMCTV.com, "Q&A - RJ Mitte (Walter Jr.)"

[29] S.B., "Color Commentary On the Names From TV's 'Breaking Bad'"

[30] *Breaking Bad* Wikia, "Mike Ehrmantraut"

[31] Genesis 17:5

[32] Genesis 32:28

[33] Acts 9:1-22

[34] Alternatively, Paul may have simply chosen to refer to himself by a Gentile name rather than a Jewish name. Since he preached the gospel to Gentiles, this would make sense as well. Luke Buckler, "Why did Paul change his name from Saul to Paul?"

[35] I was named after a fictional TV character from an 80s nighttime soap opera.

[36] Revelation 12:17b

[37] Mike Flaherty, "The Showrunner Transcript: *Breaking Bad*'s Vince Gilligan on Season Four and His Experiences on The X-Files"

[38] That is, until the last few episodes, signaling that Heisenberg has returned to being Walter White.

[39] Dustin Rowles, 'Breaking Bad' Theory: The Internet Unearths The Perfect Metaphor For Walter White's Soul

[40] Bryan Cranston on Walter White's look, Nicole LaPorte, "The 100 Most Creative People in Business 2013: 8: Bryan Cranston," *Fast Company, June 2013*

[41] Erin Enberg, "The Changing Colors of *Breaking Bad*"

[42] Called "Blue Sky" in the series, the writers intentionally ensured that Walter's meth was blue in order to make it "visually identifiable." BreakingBad.Wikia.com

[43] AMCtv.com, "*Breaking Bad* Creator Vince Gilligan Answers Fan Questions - Part II"

[44] Erin Enberg, "The Colorful World of *Breaking Bad*"

[45] AMCtv.com, Quebrando Mal, "What You're Saying About Colors on *Breaking Bad*"

[46] Alyssa Rosenberg, "*Breaking Bad* Open Thread: Wind In the Willows"

[47] Like leaving a copy of "Leaves of Grass" out on one's toilet.

[48] Pearson Moore, "Breaking Down *Breaking Bad*"

[49] To recap, Walter allowed Jesse's girlfriend Jane to die of a drug overdose. Her father, the air traffic controller on the fateful day of the collision, was so distraught over the loss of his daughter that he was unable to fulfill his high-stress duties on the job, resulting in that cataclysmic event. Lest you think this series of events might require a serious stretching of real-life possibilities, the Überlingen mid-air collision of 2002, resulting in the death of 71 people, was reported to have been caused by an over-worked air-traffic controller and technology failures. Even more shockingly, the controller at fault was consequently murdered by a father and husband who'd lost his wife and two children in the crash. Wikipedia, Überlingen mid-air collision.

[50] "Vince Gilligan has made it clear that the pink teddy bear of Season Two is an homage to Steven Spielberg's Girl in the Red Coat in *Schindler's List*." — Pearson Moore, "Breaking Down *Breaking Bad*". In that movie, the red coat is the only object in color, a symbol of the girl's innocence and the Jews' innocence during the Holocaust. The titular character later sees the girl in a mound of dead bodies that have been exhumed. Innocence

has died.

[51] Erin Enberg, "The Changing Colors of *Breaking Bad*"

[52] Will Harris, "*Breaking Bad*'s Betsy Brandt on the evolution of her character"

[53] Infographic, "The Final Death Toll in *Breaking Bad*"

[54] This number skews high because of the collision of the Wayfarer 515 and JM 21 flights in the final episode of Season 2.

[55] In Season 5, Episode 2's "Madrigal," Mike Erhmanntraut even tells Walter, "You are a time bomb, tick-tick-ticking," just in case anyone watching the show wasn't already greatly aware of that fact.

[56] R.J. Mitte, the actor who plays Walter White Jr., lives with a milder form of cerebral palsy than does his character. In fact, he reportedly had to learn how to augment his CP as the series progressed and his character received more screen time.

[57] Later in the same episode, while on a DEA bust of Jesse "Cap'n Cook" Pinkman's meth lab, Hank tells Walt that if a meth lab mix goes wrong, you could create mustard gas. Apparently, Walter can't escape the deadly condiment.

[58] A good thing to do in a pilot episode, by the way.

[59] Vince Gilligan and his writers are insidious in the ways they portray the dual natures of Walter White so quickly in succession. This is on purpose, of course, and will be discussed in a later chapter.

[60] AMCtv.com, "*Breaking Bad* Creator Vince Gilligan Answers Fan Questions - Part II"

[61] If you're a fan of the show, you would do well to pick up Chris Seay's *The Gospel According to Tony Soprano* and Alan Sepinwall's *The Revolution was Televised*.

[62] *Breaking Bad* paid subtle homages to *The Sopranos*. One of the members of the Juárez drug cartel was called Juan Bolsa, which translates to "Johnny Sack," a character in *The Sopranos*. Additionally, Season 5's opener "Live Free or Die" was also the title of a *Sopranos* episode (as well as being the state motto of New Hampshire). Dustin Rowles, "20 Neat Facts, Cool Allusions, Instances Of Foreshadowing, And Theories On 'Breaking Bad.'"

[63] 1 Corinthians 15:26

[64] 1 Corinthians 15:55

[65] Had humanity remained perfect and continued to multiply with all of us physically living for eternity is a question for smarter men than me to consider.

[66] Yes, I just quoted *Quantum Leap*, but you're reading *a footnote*

in a book about God and Walter White, so judge not lest ye be judged.

[67] It may also occur as Mike's ultimate penance for the misdeeds that have characterized his life for so long.

[68] Proverbs 16:25

[69] In an intricately woven plot detail, it should be noted that Gustavo Fring was not above using children to carry out his own evil plans. In fact, Andrea's brother, 11-year-old Tomas, was used to kill Combo as part of a gang initiation, a gang reported to be working for Fring. Combo was a dealer for Heisenberg in Season 2, as well as the contract through which Walter and Jesse found their unmistakable RV, which previously belonged to Combo's mother.

[70] "I am the one who rings!"

[71] Barring the fact, of course, that you are a real person and Walter White is not.

[72] Andrew Romano, "'Breaking Bad' Creator Vince Gilligan Reveals the Finale Will Be 'Victorious'"

[73] Michka Assayas, *Bono: In Conversation with Michka Assayas*

[74] If this topic intrigues you, I recommend David T. Lamb's *God Behaving Badly: Is the God of the Old Testament Angry, Sexist and Racist?*

[75] Billy Coffey, "Fisher of Men"

[76] The narcissistic tendencies we tend to see on reality TV result in a strange, redundant vortex of narcissism, i.e. narcissists are likely to be on reality TV as "the dramatic ones" because their inability to see themselves for who they truly are manages to cause great stress and conflict, one of the necessary aspects of an engaging narrative.

[77] Bryan Cranston, "Bryan Cranston Picks 13 Favorite 'Breaking Bad' Moments"

[78] Proverbs 16:18

[79] Lane Brown, "In Conversation: Vince Gilligan on the End of Breaking Bad"

[80] C.S. Lewis, *Mere Christianity*

[81] A few caveats: Walter is directly responsible for five deaths prior to the last eight episodes of the series. In the pilot episode, he gasses Emilio in the RV. In Season 1, Episode 3, he strangles Krazy-8. In Season 3, Episode 12, he famously saves Jesse from an imminent demise by running down rival drug dealers with his menacing Pontiac Aztek. Lastly, in Season 5, Episode 7, Walter surprisingly shoots Mike Ehrmantraut. Considering that he's indirectly responsible for 268 deaths, his percentage for actually committing a murder is quite low at just 2%.

[82] The Battle at Kruger has been viewed more than 70 million times. In this somewhat gruesome video, a pride of lions attack a baby water buffalo, but it ends well, all things considered.

[83] Are all of Walter's actions a reaction to his cancer diagnosis? Does he set out, even subconsciously so, to exact his revenge on God by attempting to poison the world he currently resides in?

[84] Of course, all of them have suffered some type of deep, emotional wound, but you see such wounds much more clearly in the case of the latter three mentioned here.

[85] You may not have felt compassion at the fact that Hayden Christensen was the one suffering, but that's on you.

[86] One could also argue that so much death occurs in our movies simply because death ratchets the stakes higher in any film. Without death, what are the heroes really fighting for?

[87] A contemporary imagining of the punishment Satan faces in Dante's *Inferno*.

[88] Martin Miller, "The end nears for Walter White of 'Breaking Bad'"

[89] Andrew Romano, "'Breaking Bad' Creator Vince Gilligan Reveals the Finale Will Be 'Victorious'"

[90] Alyssa Rosenberg, "'Breaking Bad' Open Thread: Wind in the

Willows"

[91] Richard Rene, *Breaking Bad, or How to Go to Hell in Five Award-Winning Seasons*"

[92] The embroidered pillow boldly and darkly proclaims "Find Joy in the Little Things."

[93] That said, I still didn't think Walter would die in the finale, as you read in the previous chapter.

[94] Chuck Klosterman, *"Bad* Decisions"

[95] It also helps that Jonathan Banks is a fine actor, finally nominated for an Emmy in 2013 as an Outstanding Supporting Actor in a Drama Series. Unfortunately for the voters, so was Jesse Pinkman's Aaron Paul.

[96] Of course, we know it's the writers who ultimately hold the strings, the gods of the *Breaking Bad* universe, but they make Walter appear as the master puppeteer of the series.

[97] "The thing is, if you just do stuff and nothing happens, what's it all mean? What's the point?" - Jesse in Season 4, Episode 5's "Problem Dog"

[98] Chuck Klosterman, *"Bad* Decisions"

[99] "I Am Bryan Cranston, AMA"

[100] Vince Gilligan talking to Alan Sepinwall in "Interview: 'Breaking Bad' creator Vince Gilligan post-mortems season three"

[101] *Breaking Bad: Alchemy*, iBook, pg. 6

[102] The beginning of Season 5, with Walt in a diner celebrating his 52nd birthday alone and an M60 machine gun stowed in his trunk, is the same way. As a literal "Chekhov's gun," this scene is a flash-forward that the writers reportedly devised before fully developing how Walter got from Point A to Point B. See Brett Martin's "The Last Stand of Walter White"

[103] Carl Jung, *Modern Man in Search of a Soul*

[104] Technically, the game wouldn't have existed in the *Breaking Bad* universe since it was released in 2010 and the entire series purportedly takes place circa 2008, but you can't fault the writers for taking the opportunity to use such a well-suited title for this particular episode.

[105] As an intriguing side note, the colors red, blue, and green splash on Jesse's face as he plays the game, a visual reference back to Walter's "beakers of change" in the pilot episode.

[106] In contrast, Walter wears dark clothes in this scene, insidiously manipulating Jesse by reinforcing the false idea that Gus orchestrated little Brock's poisoning.

[107] Jesse calls out the NA counselor here over the reason for the

counselor's own struggle with addiction.

[108] wiNNEBAGO, comment, "Breaking Bad: 'Problem Dog' Review"

[109] Of course, Walter, as ever, is blinded by his own ego. Jesse has a serious girlfriend, which for many is more than enough reason to step away from life-threatening endeavors.

[110] r32mara23, comment, "Breaking Bad: 'Problem Dog' Review"

[111] Jane Margolis: "Do you know what this is?"

Jesse Pinkman: "It's a whole lot of cheddar."

Jane: "This is freedom. This is saying, 'I can go anywhere I want. I can be anybody.' What do you want to be? Where do you want to go? South America? Europe? Australia?"

Jesse: "Is New Zealand part of Australia?"

Jane: "New Zealand is New Zealand."

Jesse: "Right on. New Zealand. That's where they made 'Lord of the Rings.' I say we just move there, yo. I mean, you can do your art. Right? Like, you can paint the local castles and s—. And I can be a bush pilot."

— Season 2, Episode 12, "Phoenix"

[112] Lane Brown, "In Conversation: Vince Gilligan on the End of Breaking Bad"

[113] Unless otherwise noted, the following section contains statistics and quotes from the National Geographic's *World's Most Dangerous Drug,* an hour-long documentary that provides an informative glimpse into the desperate lives of those whom meth has overtaken.

[114] Donna Leinwand, "DEA: Flavored meth use on the rise"

[115] Sobering before-and-after mugshots can be seen at "Faces of Meth."

[116] Google, "Define insidious"

[117] A methaphor, perhaps?

[118] 1 John 1:8-9

[119] George MacDonald, *The Princess and Curdie*

[120] Let him live:
It's the moral thing to do.
Judeo/Christian principles
You are not a murder.

Kill him:
He'll kill your entire family if you let him go.

[121] Shockingly and tellingly, the bloodline that ran from David and Bathsheba through their son Solomon ultimately resolved in the birth of Jesus. To look at the lives of those listed in Matthew 1 for Jesus' genealogy is to realize that God both loves and uses the morally corrupt for his greater purposes.

[122] 2 Samuel 12:1-7

[123] 2 Samuel 12:13-18

[124] Leo Tolstoy, "Pamphlets"

[125] "I Am Bryan Cranston, AMA"

[126] SaveWalterWhite.com

[127] Luke 15:11-32

[128] I was peering into the future with this comparison since the last half of the last season had yet to air as of the writing of the first edition of this book. I was wrong about Jesse sacrificing himself for Walter, but a sacrifice *did* occur by series' end. I just had the names transposed.

[129] This is to say, I believed a sacrifice *would* be made on Walter's behalf. I didn't think that Walter would die by series' end, but I thought it'd be interesting if he did so as a heroic sacrifice. However, if that happened, I thought it would negate Gilligan's intentions to turn Walt from Mr. Chips to Scarface. In many

ways, a heroic sacrifice would redeem Walter in the audience's eyes, just as a possible heroic sacrifice by Jesse would redeem all of his actions. This contrast between my expectations of the finale and what actually occurred is further considered in the last chapter, which was written after the series' finale.

[130] Brett Martin, "The Last Stand of Walter White"

[131] "Everyone who calls on the name of the Lord will be saved." - Romans 10:13

For more information on what it means to have a relationship with God, visit PeaceWithGod.net.

[132] I'm envisioning an episode called "Return of the Fly."

[133] David Auerbach, "The Cosmology of Serialized Television"

[134] According to Zap2It's TV by the Numbers, 2,781,000 viewers watched "Gliding Over All," the Season 5 mid-season finale.

[135] Lane Brown, "In Conversation: Vince Gilligan on the End of Breaking Bad"

[136] Ibid

[137] Martin Miller, "The end nears for Walter White of 'Breaking Bad'"

[138] "*Breaking Bad*: How Much Cash Was in That Storage Unit?" estimates the cash cube to equal roughly $50 million.

[139] This scene screams color coding. Notice the primary colors within the storage room: green money rests atop a red tarp, gazed upon by blue-clad Walter and Skyler.

[140] Madrigal Electromotive's home country.

[141] Dustin Rowles, "9 Open Questions At The Midpoint of 'Breaking Bad' Season 5"

[142] Dustin Rowles, "Insane 'Breaking Bad' Theory Backed By Questionable Evidence So Good It Might Be True"

[143] Dustin Rowles, "20 Neat Facts, Cool Allusions, Instances Of Foreshadowing, And Theories On 'Breaking Bad'"

[144] Brett Martin, "The Last Stand of Walter White"

[145] Hal Wilkerson was Bryan Cranston's previous comedic role in "Malcolm in the Middle."

[146] Brett Martin, "The Last Stand of Walter White"

[147] For those who thought I feared too much for baby Holly's safety prior to the last eight episodes: "We had some pretty dark days in the writers' room. No one was safe, not even baby Holly." - Vince Gilligan, The 'Breaking Bad' Finale Was Not A Dream

[148] Ben Blacker, *Fast Company, June 2013,* "The Brainiac Box," Pg. 158

[149] • Andy Greenwald, Breaking Bad Series Finale: A Man Becomes a Legend in 'Felina'
• Alan Sepinwall, Series finale review: 'Breaking Bad' - 'Felina': It's all over now, baby blue
• Kevin McFarland, 'Breaking Bad,' Season 5, Episode 16, 'Felina': review
• Adam Bryant, Breaking Bad "Felina" Recap: How Did It All End?
• Maureen Ryan, 'Breaking Bad' Finale Review, 'Felina': The Big Finish Felt Small At Times
• James, Poniewozik, Breaking Bad Watch: Say Hello to My Little Friend

[150] • Keatan Lumanog, Twitter
• Chris Somers, Twitter
• Jana Kinsman, Twitter

[151] Damon Lindelof, "Damon Lindelof on Why 'Breaking Bad's' Finale Let Him Say Goodbye to 'Lost' (Guest Column)"

[152] For what it's worth, I liked *LOST*'s ending. Additionally, have you noticed the similarities between the two shows? People yelling "Walt!" all the time, a devastating plane crash, the importance of a chicken restaurant, lottery numbers, flash forwards and flashbacks, a hatch, the notion that characters may have actually been dead at some point though still

portrayed as alive on screen ...

[153] Sara Bibel, "'Breaking Bad' Finale Scores Record 10.3 Million Viewers, 6.7 Million Adults 18-49"

[154] Many fans would have liked the series to continue, as evidenced by Jeffrey Katzenberg's incredible offer of $75 million for *Breaking Bad* to produce three more episodes for online release. — "Breaking Bad and the $75 Million Crazy Plan to Shake Up Television"

[155] Marshall Crook, "How the 'Breaking Bad' Finale Put it All Together"

[156] This disconnect could also be an unintentional jab at fathers who adamantly say that they're working so many hours for the good of their family, when in reality the best thing these men could do is work *fewer* hours in order to spend more time with their families. Even though Walter's second job has many attendant dangers to it, it's the hours that the job requires that serve to further undermine his ardent belief that he's providing for his family.

[157] Again, one of Walter's manipulations backfires on him, karmic retribution seemingly destined to out Heisenberg. Had Walter never goaded Jesse into leaving Albuquerque, Jesse would never have been in Saul's office for Huell to steal his small stash of pot from his pocket, the almost-missable moment through which Jesse ultimately learns about Walter's poisoning of Brock.

[158] Brett Martin, "The Last Stand of Walter White," GQ Magazine

[159] Dan Snierson, "'Breaking Bad': Creator Vince Gilligan explains series finale," Entertainment Weekly

[160] Emily Nussbaum, "The Closure-Happy 'Breaking Bad' Finale," The New Yorker

[161] Joyce Carol Oates, Twitter status update, October 4, 2013

[162] Norm MacDonald, Twitter status update, October 2, 2013

[163] Ibid

[164] Ibid

[165] "Vince Gilligan Tackles Four 'Breaking Bad' Myths," The Hollywood Reporter

[166] Breeanna Hare, "'Breaking Bad': Walter White laid to rest with mock funeral"

[167] As with most issues in *Breaking Bad*, this is a debatable point. I could also argue that the finale featured both Heisenberg and Walter White. They're so inextricably linked by that point that maybe Walter was trying to set himself free from Heisenberg, but he only knows how to accomplish such things in a Heisenbergian way. In other words, Walter has to manipulate

Heisenberg to accomplish Walter's ends. It's *Fight Club*.

[168] Norm MacDonald points to the statement "I was alive" as yet another clue to the "Walter's already dead" theory, literally interpreting Walter's words: he *was* alive, but it's actually dead Walter that's speaking to Skyler in this moment.

[169] At first, Gilligan's music team didn't agree with his song choice for the ending, but once they saw the dailies of the finale footage, they understood Gilligan's choice. *Breaking Bad*'s music supervisor Thomas Golubić then said, "Oh, I get it now . . . This is a love-affair story of Walt and his love of science, and this was his greatest product – his greatest triumph as a chemist. It wasn't about Walter White as a criminal or a murderer or an awful person. It was him ending on his own terms. It felt creatively right." — Steve Knopper, "Why 'Breaking Bad' Chose Badfinger's 'Baby Blue'"

[170] Ryan Reed, "'Breaking Bad' Script Leak Answers Finale Questions"

[171] Ibid

[172] If you disagree with this interpretation, read Vince Gilligan's notes on the finale's script. In describing the final scene, he writes, "[The police] move in cautiously, their guns aimed. They're too late. He got away." — Kris Maske, "Here Are The Final Two Pages Of 'Breaking Bad's' 'Felina' Series Finale Screenplay"

[173] I do not believe that our actions, whether good or bad, work to redeem us, as if we can tip the moral scales to our favor. However, within popular culture and many narratives of our day, good or bad actions are the only way we can see a person's interior motives made real.

Made in the USA
San Bernardino, CA
19 December 2013